Beginning Ancient Greek

A Visual Workbook

Fiona McPherson, PhD

Published 2020 by Wayz Press, Wellington, New Zealand.

ISBN 978-1-927166-63-5

To report errors, please email errata@wayz.co.nz
For additional resources and up-to-date information about any errors, go to the Mempowered website at www.mempowered.com

Also by Dr McPherson

Easy Russian Alphabet: A Visual Workbook

Indo-European Cognate Dictionary

Mnemonics for Study (2nd ed.)

My Memory Journal

How to Approach Learning: What teachers and students should know about succeeding in school

Successful Learning Simplified: A Visual Guide

How to Learn: The 10 principles of effective practice and revision

Effective Notetaking (3rd ed.)

Planning to Remember: How to remember what you're doing and what you plan to do

Perfect Memory Training

The Memory Key

Contents

Learning the letters

How we learn

The standard way to learn an alphabet is as a list of letters in 'alphabetical order'. As children, we learn our native alphabet 'by rote' — that is, through exact and boring repetition. Quite likely, a measure of interest and attractiveness was granted by means of rhythm or song. But still, a lot of boring repetition was needed. As adult learners, our tolerance for this sort of thing is much less! Moreover, rote repetition is a supremely inefficient means of learning.

How do we learn? Learning happens through two fundamental processes: connection, and repetition.

Well, rote repetition has the repetition part covered. But not the part that makes learning fun, not the part that speeds the process.

Connection is what holds our memory together. Connection is what enables us to search our memory and find what we're looking for. Connection is what makes information meaningful. Connection is what makes information interesting.

We always need repetition — you can't do away, entirely, with repetition. But how much you need, *that* varies a great deal. If we can make connections to information already well known to us, then that new information will be more easily remembered — meaning that it needs less repetition. For example, if your cousin has a new baby and names it Geraldine — a family name, the name of your aunt and great-aunt and great-grandmother — you will remember this much more easily than you would a less relevant name, chosen simply because the parents liked the sound of it.

When we learn meaningful topics, such as the causes of the Great War, or how black holes are formed, connections are made and strengthened in a way that reflects your growing understanding of the subject. When we learn something that is less rooted in meaning, such as vocabulary in a new language, reducing the amount of repetition required often depends on creating new, arbitrary connections.

This is the whole point of mnemonics (acronyms, images, silly stories) — to make arbitrary connections more memorable.

The corollary of that, of course, is that information that is meaningful (that is, has connections within itself and to information you already hold) doesn't need mnemonic help.

So, reducing repetition (the aim of efficient, and more enjoyable, learning) is about finding and making connections, which may be meaningful (best) or arbitrary (not as good, but still much better than the brute force of rote repetition).

Furthermore, repetition can be made more effective and enjoyable by applying a certain degree of variation, and by using optimal spacing and timing.

This book uses all these strategies — including grouping, mnemonic images, and opportunities for varied retrieval practice — in order to most efficiently and effectively learn the Greek alphabet.

Grouping for memory

It is important to know the alphabetical order, if only so that you can find words in a dictionary. However, it's better to disentangle these two tasks — learning the letters, and learning the order of the letters — so, we'll get to the alphabet after mastering each letter.

I have broken down the Greek alphabet into groups based on how difficult the letters are to learn, for native users of the Roman alphabet (which is the one used by English speakers). Doing it this way not only enables you to more quickly master the bulk of the letters, it also explicitly tells you which letters need to be practiced more.

We're going to start with the easiest group — those which are just the same in both alphabets.

You may wonder why it's necessary to spend any time at all on these letters, which obviously you already know. There are two reasons. The first, and most important, is that there are some letters that are 'false friends' — that is, they look just like English letters, but they correspond to different sounds. It is not enough, therefore, to simply recognize the letters as the ones you're used to; you need to know that these are indeed the same letters you're familiar with. (Note that from now on I will use the word 'English' as a more user-friendly term for the Roman alphabet, given that this book is written in the English language.)

The second reason is that recognizing some letters is only good for the situation where you're reading the language. To write in it, you need to go further than recognition; you need to be able to produce the right letters. This means you need to know which letters represent which sounds.

The mnemonic cards

The foundation of your learning is the visual images I've constructed for each letter. Notice that each "card" shows, first, the upper and lower case forms of the Greek letter, written in a color picked out from the picture. This is followed by the name of the letter, and then the English letter that is translated as its equivalent.

At the bottom of the card is a phrase which includes both a keyword to help you remember the letter name, plus another to remind you of the way the letter is pronounced. So, for example, in the card below, we have 'elf' as the keyword to the Greek letter name 'alpha', and the word 'car' points to the way in which this 'a' sound is pronounced. These word cues are particularly important for vowels, which can be pronounced in so many ways.

The keyword phrase is also portrayed in an image. You can focus on either the image or the phrase, depending on your preference, but in either case, you should also give some attention to the other. Images are generally more memorable than words, but this is a matter of language, after all — you need to attach

the images very firmly to their associated words, thinking 'car' when you look at or visualize the green car, and 'elf' when you look at or imagine the creature with the paintbrush.

The key to learning the letters is to build strong links between the image and the keywords and the Greek letters. I'll talk more about this as we go. For now, let's have a look at the first group. This will give you the opportunity to see the strategy at work.

Group 1: Friends

There are 7 letters in this friendliest group — friendly because the capital letters at least, and most of the lower-case letters, are identical to our own letters, and mean the same thing. Pay attention to the minor ways in which some of the lower-case letters differ from our letters, but the main thing you need to memorize from this group is the name of the letters. These images will help you do that.

A α

alpha

a

the elf paints the car

B β

beta

b

βeating the βeets

Alpha and beta are names that are probably familiar to you, so learning these will be easy, not really deserving of mnemonic keywords. The next letter, however, is likely to be much stranger to you. Not many words are going to be good cues for epsilon! But this brand name will be familiar to most. Make sure you remember that it's Pepsi, and not it's more famous competitor.

E ε

epsilon

e

Pepsi for my pεt

The iconic picture of an atom in this next image is there as a symbol for the word 'iota'. But it's hard to portray or visualize an iota, so I've instead used the keyword phrase 'eye out' to cue the letter name. Using the more familiar word 'bit' also cues you to the short 'i' pronunciation, particularly important when the word iota suggests a different pronunciation for the 'i'.

Iι

iota

i

Just a bit, but it nearly took my eye out

It's a little confusing, because in English 'c' can be pronounced 'hard' (k) or 'soft' (s), but 'cap' is such a good keyword for kappa that it's hard to go past it. The kangaroo will remind you that it really is a 'k'. The use of graduate's cap is a head-nod to a use of the word 'kappa' that may be familiar to Americans — as part of a college fraternity name.

Κκ

kappa

k

A cap for a kangaroo

The next one is another strange sounding name. You could work something out with the keyword 'micro', but that's a pretty abstract word, and I've instead gone with the somewhat lengthy phrase 'home with Mike and Ron', which has the virtue of using very familiar words. Note that the letter is pronounced as a short 'o', as in 'hot'. Again, this is in contrast to the pronunciation signal given the word itself.

Οo

omicron

o

Hot at home with Mike & Ron

The final letter in this group is short and snappy, and may be familiar to some of you through physics (tau particles) or health/medicine (tau proteins).

Pay attention to the differences — or lack of them — between the upper- and lower-case letters. In particular, note that for kappa and tau, unlike their counterparts

Ττ

tau

t

The tall tower

in English, the lower-case letters are simply smaller versions of the upper-case letters.

Remembering that it's useful to know which letters are true friends and which false friends, you might find it helpful to use the acronym I ABET OK to remember which letters belong in this group.

> To remember which letters are the same in both languages, use the mnemonic: **I ABET OK**

How to practice

Mnemonic images and stories do help enormously, but if you look at them once and never again, they're going to fade from your mind quickly enough. You do need to rehearse them.

Which doesn't mean looking at them repeatedly! You need to actually retrieve them from your memory. This is a basic principle of learning: **only practice that involves retrieving items from your long-term memory helps you remember!**

The review sections, then, provide exercises for you to do this.

Calling them "reviews" is a little misleading, because they are not just a means to test your learning, but also a means of practicing *for* learning. How much practice you'll need will vary with the group — this first group should require very little. However, it's important to note that it's not simply a matter of getting the answers correct. Because letters need to be over-learned to the point of automaticity (so that you don't need to wonder, even fleetingly, what a letter is), you want to return to these reviews again and again, until you can answer them correctly instantly, without thought.

Variation is definitely a part of effective practice, which is why I provide another type of practice. After each review, you will find vocabulary sections, listing words that are mostly very similar to their English counterparts. (Some words may be harder to guess, but you can check out their meaning in the Glossary at the back of the book.) Practice reading these words at intervals, until you are completely fluent.

A word about timing: a key factor in practicing effectively, with number of repetitions kept to the minimum necessary for long-term retention, is how you space your practice sessions. The basic rules are:

- review three times at increasingly spaced intervals

- only successful reviews count

- the spacing should occur just before you are about to forget without review

- as a rule of thumb (since that is tricky to calculate until you've become more familiar with your own learning skills):

  - review for the first time one day after learning

  - 2nd review a week or so later

  - 3rd review a month after that

- it's better to space your reviews longer than too short — make your brain work for it.

Although this book emphasizes reading, which is about recognition (a much easier level of memory to acquire than recall), nevertheless you can help your learning by practicing yet another type of variation — that of writing. Writing the letters means the involvement of muscle memory, which as we all know is a very potent form of memory indeed.

Greek letters are good doodling material, but to get you off to a good start, I'm including some letters to trace. They'll be scattered through the book.

α α α α α α α α α α α α α

β β β β β β β β β β β β

ε ε ε ε ε ε ε ε ε ε ε ε ε

Review 1.1

1. What's the mnemonic for remembering the letters that are exactly the same in Greek and English?

    a. Elf in a Tower

    b. ATOM K

    c. Elf gives kangaroo hot beets and a Pepsi

    d. I ABET OK

2. Match the Greek letters to their associated images.

    O I T A B E

3. Pick the Greek letter that corresponds to English letter b:

    a. κ

    b. o

    c. β

    d. α

4. Pick the name for the Greek letter ι:

    a. kappa

    b. alpha

    c. tau

    d. iota

5. Pick the Greek letter that corresponds to English letter o:

   a. τ

   b. α

   c. ε

   d. o

6. Pick the Greek letter that corresponds to English letter e:

   a. o

   b. β

   c. α

   d. ε

7. Match the Greek letters to their associated images.

ι τ β o κ ε

8. Pick the English letter that corresponds to Greek letter α:

   a. o

   b. e

   c. a

   d. b

9. Pick the English letter that corresponds to Greek letter omicron:

    a. o

    b. t

    c. e

    d. k

10. Pick the name for the Greek letter τ:

    a. beta

    b. tau

    c. epsilon

    d. iota

Vocabulary

You only know a few letters so far, so our vocabulary list is necessarily very short! Don't worry, the lists quickly increase in size, giving you plenty of opportunities for practice.

Here are ten easy Greek words, using the letters you now know:

αἰεί	το
ἐκ	οἱ
εἰ	ὅτι
και	τί
κακοι	καιτοι

Don't worry about the accent marks above some of the vowels at the moment.

Although in general I've avoided including vocabulary that have no obvious connections to English words, these words are so short and basic they tend to lack such links. The collected vocabulary lists in the Glossary include meanings, along with clues to help you remember them. I haven't put those here, because your focus should be on instantly recognizing the letters, and being able to read the words as easily as you do English.

On this first occasion, read the words over as many times as you need, until the letters come fluently — an easy enough task for this first group, but it will get harder with subsequent lists. When you're satisfied with your fluency, check the list with the meanings. Note which words are exactly as expected, and which are not (in this first list, none of them are likely to be expected, but this will change in subsequent lists, when the words can be longer). Read the clues, if any, and see whether they make sense for you — our minds are all different, reflecting our different experiences, so what helps me will not necessarily help you. But my suggestion may spark a different connection for you. Go with it.

When you're learning, and on subsequent reviews, the same 'rule of 3' applies — each word needs to be read easily 3 times.

Note that the fluency you've attained in reading the list the first time is illusory. The words are still fresh in your mind. They haven't yet been transferred to long-term memory. So however easy and obvious they seem, don't forget your reviews. On your reviews, try to read the words for meaning as well.

Spacing your practice

There's a happy line between learning too fast and learning too slow. If you speed through this book too fast, you risk fooling yourself with learning that isn't properly consolidated, and won't necessarily be there when you need it later. You're also more likely to develop confusions between some letters. On the other hand, if you work through the book too slowly, your learning won't feed on itself, and will be much slower (that is, learning will actually be slower, not simply take more time).

At the very end of the book, after the Collected Vocabulary Lists, I have a complete list of the words in alphabetical order. This list doesn't include meanings or transcriptions. It is your final review list. Once you've worked your way through all the letters, use this list for any further reviews.

I suggest you do your first two reviews (at one day and one week) of each list using that list, but use the complete list for your 3rd (and any subsequent) reviews. This will work well if you've got through the lists at a reasonable pace, but if you're slow, you might need to do your 3rd review using the individual lists.

Here's a sample guide to the pace, just to give you the idea:

Day 1: **learn Group 1**

Day 2: **learn Group 2; review Group 1**

Day 3: **review Group 2; learn Group 3** (assuming you find Groups 1 & 2 easy)

Day 4: **review Group 3**

Day 5: if Group 3 review didn't go well, repeat it

Day 6: if all learning has gone well, **learn Group 4**

Day 7: **review Group 4**

Day 8: Group 4 is tricky — even if you did well in the previous review, run through the quick practice to make sure you've got them mastered; if everything is going well, **start learning Group 5**

Day 9: **review Group 1** (2nd review — remember, only successful reviews count!); continue learning Group 5

Day 10: **review Group 2** (2nd review); **review Group 5**

Day 11: **review Group 3** (2nd review)

Day 13: run through the quick practice for Group 5 (assuming the previous review went well)

Day 14: **review Group 4** (2nd review)

Day 16: **review Group 5** (2nd review)

Day 46: **complete review** (3rd review)

That all might seem a little over-complicated and intimidating! Don't panic, it's just an illustration, to give you the shape of the process. Note that your learning 'session' might be spread over more than one day, if you're finding a group difficult. What that means, essentially, is that rather than doing a simple review (run through of the vocabulary list), you study the cards again and repeat the test, as well as practicing on the vocab list. You may find it useful to use the 'Quick practice' cards too (you'll see them later, when the letters get more challenging).

You will realize that the early groups inevitably get practiced in the later vocabulary lists; this reduces the need for a formal 3rd review. However, that's not perfect. Once you have all the letters mastered, you can then use the complete list for a 3rd review. You may also feel the need for further reviews.

Individuals vary in their learning abilities in different areas. What's easy for one may be difficult for another. The 'rule of 3' is a guideline. If you remember this type of information easily, you might only need to repeat words twice; if you find this type of learning difficult, you might need to repeat and review four or more times.

Moreover, the words themselves make a difference. Easy words, such as the ones in this list, might only need to be covered twice by everyone. The point is to be sensitive to your own learning. Experience will tell you what works for you.

You may find it helpful to use a table like this one on the next page, to help you keep track of where you are.

	Review 1	Quick practice	Review 2	Review 3
Group 1				
Group 2				
Group 3				
Group 4				
Group 5				
Full list				

Group 2: Near-friends

In this small group of near friends, the upper-case letters are again identical to their counterparts in our alphabet, but this time the lower-case letters are very different.

This lower-case z is not, however, as strange as it may seem on first glance — not, at least, for those who learned handwriting. Here is the English lower-case z, written in what is now called cursive:

Z ζ

zeta

z

let the cheetah snooζe!

Even for those familiar with this version of the English letter, the Greek letter does require practice. Do make sure you physically practice drawing all those forms that are unfamiliar to you — even if you don't intend ever to write in Greek, muscle memory is a very durable memory, so physically drawing the letters is an excellent way to practice.

With this next letter, note that the lower-case letter is very like a 'u'. This fits in very nicely with the name of the letter, so you can use that to remind you of the form of the lower-case m (do note the way the left-hand 'stick' drops below the line).

M μ

mu

m

a moose may 'μoo'

Interestingly, in the same way that lower-case m looks like a u, so the lower-case n looks like a v. The mnemonic *A new baby is naive* might help you remember that.

N ν

nu

n

A νew baby!

More on practice

Practice recalling your mnemonic phrases and images at idle moments such as when you're waiting in line or sitting vacantly on a bus, or resting. I like using the time before I go to sleep, or when I wake during the night, though some may find the activity too stimulating. But this time of day is particularly good for practicing information you want to learn, as it encourages the brain to pay more attention to it, when it's busy processing the day's events during sleep.

Sleep is when the brain chooses which information is worth remembering, and consolidates those memories. So any information or events you run through your mind late in the evening is more likely to be considered worthy, and consolidated (made into a long-term memory).

This is another reason for batching the letters: practice each group in turn, and don't move on until you're confident that you have a reasonable grasp of the letters. They don't have to be totally mastered though, because you'll be reviewing them later, and that's the most important part of the learning process.

You may think that, for that reason, it would be more effective to start with the most difficult letters, and that would be true if it was just a matter of practice effectiveness. But we also have to take into account psychology! Many people would be put off by starting with the most difficult letters, partly because of their difficulty, and partly because they wouldn't have sufficient skill in the learning strategies. Better to get comfortable with the strategies using the easiest letters, which are quickly mastered, before getting into deeper waters.

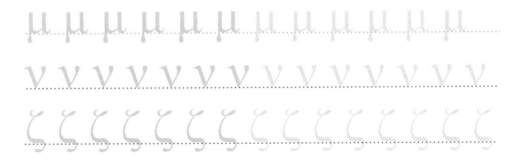

Review 1.2

1. Which of these images represents the Greek letter omicron?

2. Pick the English letter corresponding to the Greek letter ι:

    a. j

    b. g

    c. i

    d. L

3. Pick the English letter corresponding to the Greek letter epsilon:

    a. C

    b. P

    c. E

    d. I

4. Which of these images represents the
   Greek letter alpha?

5. Pick the English letter corresponding to the Greek letter kappa:

   a. c

   b. k

   c. a

   d. p

6. Pick the English letter corresponding to the Greek letter ε:

   a. e

   b. E

   c. K

   d. i

7. Which of these images represents the Greek letter tau?

8. Pick the English letter corresponding to the Greek letter β:

   a. D

   b. d

   c. B

   d. b

9. Pick the English letter corresponding to the Greek letter nu:

   a. M

   b. U

   c. V

   d. N

10. Which of these images represents the Greek letter mu?

11. Pick the English letter corresponding to the Greek letter ζ:

   a. g

   b. z

   c. f

   d. t

12. Pick the English letter corresponding to the Greek letter v:

   a. v

   b. u

   c. n

   d. Y

13. Which of these images represents the Greek letter kappa?

14. Pick the English letter corresponding to the Greek letter beta:

    a. B

    b. Z

    c. A

    d. T

15. Pick the English letter corresponding to the Greek letter zeta:

    a. E

    b. S

    c. T

    d. Z

Vocabulary

Here are 22 Greek words to practice on:

ἐν	εἶναι
το αἰμα	κατά
ὄνομᾰ	ἀνά
μέ	μανίᾱ
ἐμέ	ἀνομία
ὄμμα	μετά
ἑκατόν	ἐννέα
μιμέομαι	μεῖον
ἄντα	οἰκονομῐᾱ
ὄζειν	ἀμνίον
ἀντί	μᾰντείᾱ

What you need to know about accents & breathings

In general, the accent marks are thought to indicate pitch rather than stress — that is, a matter of melody rather than emphasis. An acute accent (´) indicates a high pitch; a circumflex (^) indicates a falling pitch; a grave accent (`) indicates a low pitch. This is not something you need to worry about if your aim is simply to read Classical Greek. (Note that, in modern Greek, the accents generally stay the same, but now indicate stress rather than pitch.)

However, you do need to notice marks at the beginning of the word, because these are 'breathings' rather than accents. Breathings indicate whether or not the vowel (and these only occur when a word begins with a vowel) is aspirated or not — that is, whether it starts with an 'h' sound.

If you study the above list, you'll see most of the words that begin with a vowel have what looks like an apostrophe above the first vowel. This means it's 'normal' — no aspiration. But if you look at ἑκατόν, you'll see that the apostrophe is now reversed. This backward hook indicates that there is an h sound at the beginning, and so ἑκατόν is transcribed as hekaton. This is important, because the meanings and connections of the word will make more sense.

Note that when the word begins with a capital letter, the mark is put first, rather than above: Ἡρακλῆς (Heracles).

You will probably also have noticed that two of the words in the above list begin with vowels but don't have breathing marks on the first vowel. This is because they begin with a diphthong (two vowels that are tied together). Where there is a diphthong, the mark appears above the second vowel.

Finally, you will have noticed that some words have two marks above the first vowel. This is because it requires both a breathing and an accent.

Group 3: False friends

This small group of 4 are false friends — they look like familiar letters (at least in their upper-case versions), but their counterparts in our alphabet are very different. You could remember that these are pretending what they're not with the acronym: HaPpY X.

Pay special attention to the phrase for H, which is another e — but a longer, more open sound. Say 'pet' and 'hair' several times, listening closely to the way the ai is pronounced in hair, and how it differs from the e in pet.

H η

eta

e

Won't eat hηr!

Again, the lower-case form is rather different — still a false friend, but this time it's echoing an n rather than an H. Like the lower-case mu (μ), which differed from our u by having a lengthened left-hand stick, the n-like letter also has a lengthened stick, this time on the right-hand side. The mnemonic phrase *Won't eat hair* will help you link the letter name and the sound of the letter. A further link to strengthen this connection will come if you look at the image in the right way — see how the high chair mimics the shape of the lower-case η, and the hook at the top of the short right-hand stick echoes the hair flying off the plate.

There is a slight complication from the sound 'hair' not being one English speakers associate with an e on its own (although vowel sounds do vary with accent, and it may be that your own way of speaking will provide a good example of an e making this sound in a word). You could extend the mnemonic phrase to *'E won't eat hair* to remind yourself that the letter is transliterated as e. (It may seem as if these mnemonic phrases have too much going on, with the letter name, the English transliteration, and the pronunciation, all being included, but it really is no problem as long as the phrase is meaningful and you keep the various associations clear in your mind as you remember the phrase / image.)

The next letter is particularly difficult, I feel, in that the incorrect answer is so obvious. Both forms of the Greek letter are identical to English letter P, and yet the letter actually represents an R — which, to make it worse, is very similar to P in appearance, and very close in the alphabet. But the phrase *row, Piper, row* should keep you straight.

P ρ

rho

r

ρow, Piper, ρow

Y υ

upsilon

u

You! I'm upside-long!

In this next letter, the lower-case letter is actually a good match for the English transliteration, but the upper-case form is a false friend.

To further complicate the matter, the name of the letter is another strange word — very like the previous one we learned. You'll need to pay particular attention that **u**psilon is not **e**psilon! I had to make up a new compound word for this keyword, but I think it's quite appropriate. (The upside-down turtle image also echoes the υ shape.)

In the final one of these false friends, the lower-case form is very similar to the upper-case (just remember that it drops below the line), and the letter name is one that will be familiar to many. However, you may think of that letter name as chee(p); instead, you should pronounce it more like the keyword 'kite'.

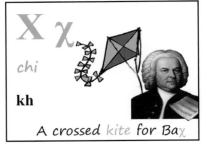

X χ

chi

kh

A crossed kite for Baχ

The pronunciation for this letter is that back of the throat sound heard in Scottish loch or German Bach (as in Johann Sebastian). Although more usually written as 'ch', 'kh' is probably a better match for the sound. You may see it transliterated as either.

We've covered over half the letters in the Greek alphabet now — the easy half. Before delving into deeper waters, do make sure that you've got a solid grasp of the letters so far. To help you with that, here they are all together. First, the upper-case letters (the easiest set — put together this way, you can

A B E Z H

I K M N O

P T Y X

see that these are all familiar letters, even if they don't all mean what they seem to mean), then the lower-case letters:

This is a good opportunity to study these lower-case letters again. Note the ways in which they differ from the English letters they resemble. Note that kappa and tau are smaller versions of the English upper-case forms, not the lower-case letters. Pay particular attention to the differences between μ, ν, and υ.

Make sure these are all solidly in your brain before moving on to the next group.

Review 1.3

1. Pick the English letter that corresponds to Greek letter P:

    a. P

    b. D

    c. R

    d. B

2. For the following images, pick the Greek letter associated with them:

    A   M   H   P   Z   Y

3. Pick the English letter that corresponds to Greek letter upsilon:

    a. L

    b. U

    c. E

    d. Y

4. Pick the English letter that corresponds to Greek letter alpha:

    a. f

    b. a

    c. L

    d. P

5. Pick the Greek letter that corresponds to English letter e:

    a. ι

    b. υ

    c. β

    d. ε

6. Pick the English letter that corresponds to Greek letter eta:

    a. H

    b. E

    c. Z

    d. B

7. For the following images, pick the Greek letter associated with them:

μ X N E υ ι

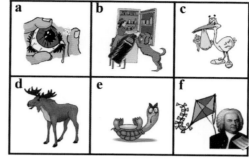

8. Pick the English letter that corresponds to Greek letter H:

   a. H

   b. E

   c. B

   d. N

9. Pick the English letter that corresponds to Greek letter μ:

   a. n

   b. p

   c. u

   d. m

10. Pick the Greek letter that corresponds to English letter n:

   a. ν

   b. υ

   c. μ

   d. η

11. Pick the English letter that corresponds to Greek letter rho:

a. B

b. R

c. P

d. F

12. For the following images, pick the Greek letter associated with them:

B ζ ν T χ K

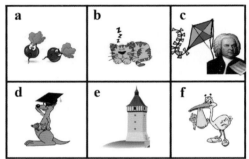

13. Pick the English letter that corresponds to Greek letter nu:

a. M

b. U

c. H

d. N

14. Pick the English letter that corresponds to Greek letter Y:

a. Y

b. U

c. I

d. T

15. What's the mnemonic for remembering the letters that are "false friends"?

 a. I ABET OK

 b. ATOM K

 c. HaPpY X

 d. HiPpY

16. Pick the English letter that corresponds to Greek letter ν:

 a. v

 b. u

 c. n

 d. m

17. Pick the English letter that corresponds to Greek letter υ:

 a. v

 b. u

 c. n

 d. m

18. For the following images, pick the Greek letter associated with them:

ρ Ο α η Ι ε

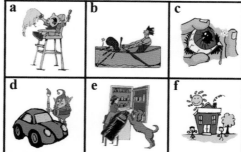

19. Pick the English letter that corresponds to Greek letter X:

   a. K

   b. X

   c. KH

   d. C

20. Pick the English letter that corresponds to Greek letter epsilon:

   a. E

   b. Z

   c. A

   d. U

Vocabulary

We now have enough letters to create more words. This means we can have more than one list, so that you can practice and review using different sets of words. Just use the first list on your initial learning session.

List 1

ἀνήρ	χαρά
μήτηρ	κῆρ
κρανίον	ἁμαρτή
ἀρετή	ἁρμονία
βᾰρεῖᾰ	βιοτή
ἄρα	νέκταρ

ὅραμα   ἀήρ
ναυτία   ὄρυζα
χᾰρᾰκτήρ   βακτηρία
τέχνη   ἑκατόμβη

List 2

αὖ   μήνη
βάκτρον   ἀράχνη
μάμμη   μέτρον
ἄρτι   αὔρᾱ
κάρα   ῥεῦμα
ὕαινα   αὖτε
χήρ   ἡμι-
νεῦρον   τρι-
ῥίζα   αὐτάρ
χάρμα   ἔντερον

List 3

ἅρμα   βοτάνη
κέντρον   ἔμβρῠον
ταὐτο   ἄημι
νάρκη   τραῦμα
ζύμη   οὖρον

Quick practice

Use these cards to quickly practice these tricky letters. The mnemonic image reminds you of the sound of the letter and its transcription — you want to build a strong link between this image and the Greek letter, so that when you see, for example, an H, you automatically think of the child in the high chair waving his bowl of hair around and crying *Won't eat it*, and from there, connect it both to the 'hair' sound and thence the English e, and the name eta.

To practice these, then, you simply look at the card, and say to yourself: "not eat hair, e, eta", "piper row, r, rho", "upside-long, u, upsilon" (you may prefer to just use the familiar word upside-down — as long as it's sufficient for you to remember the word upsilon, that's fine), "Bach with kite, X, chi". Your aim is to practice this (over time) until your responses are reliably automatic — which means that no thought is required.

Now, I know it will be tempting to cut out the additional step of remembering the object — why not simply look at the H, and say E? But the object image has much greater memorability. Including it will create a more durable memory, and it will be easier to remember.

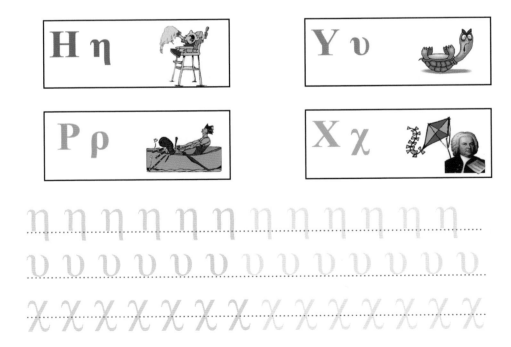

Group 4: Strange but matching

In this group of 5, although the Greek letters are quite unlike any in our own alphabet, the lower-case letters at least match their upper-case counterparts, so that the amount of memorization is reduced. Moreover, the letters are all used in science and mathematics, so may well be familiar to you.

theta

th

stuck in the tar! Θanks!

If you're not familiar with the theta character, try using this mnemonic image to impress the shape on your mind:

In the next letter, notice how the lower-case form differs from the upper-case, with the lengthening of the right-hand stroke.

How to connect the Greek letter forms with the lamb? In the following image, I show how the upper-case Λ echoes the shapes of the bell and the lamb's feet.

Λ λ

lambda

l

Λook at the lamb, da

When you study the above mnemonic card, try to see that shape superimposed on the lamb's bell and feet.

This next lower-case letter should be familiar to everyone, but note the way in which the upper-case form is more rigid. More importantly, the purple pie connects Greek letter pi to English letter p. This connection will help strengthen your mind against the false friend P (rho).

Π π

pi

p

Purple πie

The following letter is used as a symbol in math and science, but will not be as familiar to most of us.

If you're not familiar with this character, try this mnemonic image to help you with its shape:

Φ φ

phi

ph

Fight *that* φone!

The next letter is sometimes used as a symbol for psychology, psychiatry, or ESP (extrasensory perception), making this image particularly appropriate:

If you need help remembering the shape of this character, or associating the shape with the name, focus on the candelabra, which mimics the shape:

Ψ ψ

psi

ps

Maψ for a psychic

λ λ λ λ λ λ λ λ λ λ λ λ λ λ

π π π π π π π π π π π π π π

θ θ θ θ θ θ θ θ θ θ θ θ θ θ

φ φ φ φ φ φ φ φ φ φ φ φ φ

ψ ψ ψ ψ ψ ψ ψ ψ ψ ψ ψ

Review 1.4

1. For the following images, pick the Greek letter associated with them:

psi   lambda   phi

chi   pi   theta

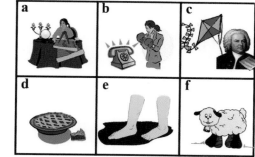

2. Pick the English letter that corresponds to Greek letter B:

   a. F

   b. P

   c. V

   d. B

3. Which of these images represents the Greek letter Φ?

4. Pick the English letter that corresponds to Greek letter λ:

   a. d

   b. y

   c. i

   d. l

5. Pick the English letter that corresponds to Greek letter ψ:

   a. ph

   b. ps

   c. ch

   d. th

6. For the following images, pick the Greek letter associated with them:

Λ   Φ   Ψ   Ρ   Θ   Υ

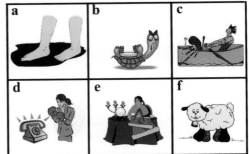

7. Pick the Greek letter that corresponds to English letter u:

   a. υ

   b. μ

   c. ψ

   d. ν

8. Pick the English letter that corresponds to Greek letter Θ:

   a. zh

   b. ch

   c. ph

   d. th

9. Pick the English letter that corresponds to Greek letter π:

   a. p

   b. r

   c. ph

   d. ps

10. For the following images, pick the Greek letter associated with them:

   beta   zeta   eta   theta

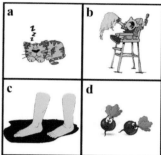

11. Pick the Greek letter that corresponds to English letter i:

   a. λ

   b. υ

   c. ι

   d. ε

12. Pick the Greek letter that corresponds to English letter p:

   a. π

   b. β

   c. φ

   d. ρ

13. Pick the name for the Greek letter ζ:

    a. beta

    b. tau

    c. zeta

    d. upsilon

14. For the following images, pick the Greek letter associated with them:

θ κ N χ M η

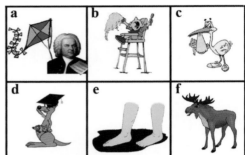

15. Pick the name for the Greek letter Ψ:

    a. phi

    b. chi

    c. psi

    d. mu

Vocabulary

List 1

ὑπέρ	πλοῖον
ἀπό	ἧπαρ
ὀνομᾰτοποιΐᾱ	πῖνον
πατήρ	φῦλον
φρᾱτηρ	κλίμα
φυή	ποτήρῐον
θυγάτηρ	κλίνη
ἄρθρον	πολεμεῖν
πέταλον	πλευρά
ψάλλειν	φύλλον

List 2

τῆλε	πρόβλημᾰ
πέτομαι	τΰμπᾰνον
ἄνᾰφορᾱ́	θύρα
φῡλή	πετάννῡμι
ἄποθήκη	θηρῐον
βῑβλῐοθήκη	φήρ
θέμα	βουλῑμία
ἠθολογῐᾱ	Πάν
θεοκρᾱτῐᾱ	χίλιοι
μύλη	κεφαλή

List 3

λίνον	μᾰκροθῡμίᾱ
θήρ	πομπή
πρωΐ	αἰθήρ
ὑπό	πῦρ
τέφρα	φορά
πτερόν	πέρᾱ
φαινόμενον	φυτόν
παραβολή	πέρᾱν
ἆθλον	ψυχή
πέντε	θηλή

List 4

τράπεζα	πιέζειν
πάλιν	πνεῦμα
λᾰλῐᾱ́	ποίημα
ἐποχή	πτυχή
φάρμακον	θαῦμα
ἑπτά	πύλη
περί	θέρμη
θέατρον	τροφή
πρίν	πέπερι
φρήν	πόρνη

Quick practice

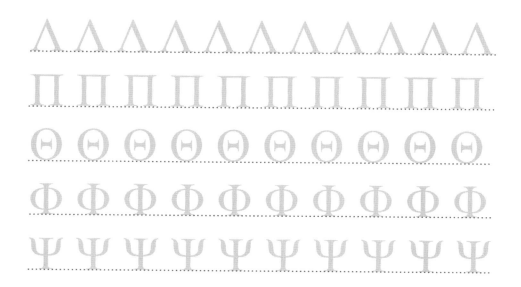

Group 5: Strangest

Here in this final group of 5, the upper-case and lower-case pairs are quite different from each other, giving you two characters to learn for each letter. However, some of the letters may well be familiar to you from science or mathematics, or general usage.

Γ γ

gamma

g

Grandma dancing
with the γoat

The goat is not really necessary, but serves to emphasize the English transliteration. Its main function, though, is to provide the mnemonic image for remembering the shapes of these letters.

Notice how the picture of the grandma dancing echoes the shape of the lower-case gamma;

see how the upper-case gamma looks like a gallows.

The name of the next letter will be familiar to most, as the word is used in several contexts, including:

- as a roughly triangular area of flat land where a river splits into multiple small rivers before spilling into the sea — examples are the Nile delta and the Mississippi delta

- as the shape of a type of airplane wing

- as the name of an American airline.

Δ δ

delta

d

δown on the river *delta*

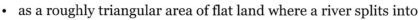

If the forms of this letter aren't familiar to you from mathematics, focus on how the lower-case delta is simply a much curvier d, while the upper-case is a triangle, as indicated by the jet plane's delta wing, or the river delta.

As is common with Greek letters, the next letter is used in math and science, but probably won't be familiar to most of us. The letter name rhymes with eye; the initial letter is usually pronounced as a z or s, in

English. Take special care not to confuse this letter with chi!

How to fix these odd shapes in your mind? Imagine the skier continuing the

fall she seems on the edge of. Imagine her tipping over so her skis form a floor and ceiling for her horizontal body. Impress upon your mind the way the skis are longer than her body. Now imagine that as she tilts over, her ax spins out of her hand and corkscrews into the air.

The next upper-case letter is probably familiar to you from school math — it's the symbol for summation. If you're not familiar with this, you might have to make a special effort not to read it as an E.

A complication with sigma is that it has two lower-case forms. There is no obvious physical correspondence between any of them! The second lower-case letter is very similar to s, but do note that the top half is much bigger than the shortened bottom half, which doesn't sit on the line but drops below it. This letter is only used at the end of words.

Notice where the two lower-case forms appear in the mnemonic phrase. See how the snail is lying upside-down on the couch, so its form mimics the first lower-case sigma. The end-of-word sigma is close enough to an English s not to need any help, but if you aren't already familiar with the upper-case sigma, you could imagine the slug tipping its head on one side, its raised eyebrows sticking up to form a bump between the prongs of his 'antlers':

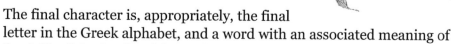

The final character is, appropriately, the final letter in the Greek alphabet, and a word with an associated meaning of 'last', 'final' (as in, the alpha and omega). Note that this letter is transliterated as o, as omicron is. You'll recall that omicron is pronounced like the o in 'hot'. Omega, on the other hand, is pronounced as a longer sound, like the aw in 'saw'. It's worth noting that omicron and omega both begin with o, followed by a word indication size: o-mega (great o); o-micron (little o).

omega

o

Should he sω the megaphone?

You may well be familiar with the upper-case shape from math or science, or from various trademarks (most famously, Omega watches). If not, concentrate how the shape is almost an O on a stand — remember that the O is open at the base.

The lower-case form is also used in math and science, but the tricky thing here is to link the character (which resembles an English w) with an 'o', and with the name omega. Focus on the sound the 'o' makes (a<u>w</u>) to help you link the w-shape with o. See how the ω-shape is echoed in the saw's handle and its edge:

Review 1.5

1. For the following images, pick the Greek letter associated with them

Ξ Σ Ψ γ Υ δ

2. Pick the name for the Greek letter Γ:

a. tau

b. epsilon

c. gamma

d. upsilon

3. Pick the name for the Greek letter Ξ:

   a. sigma

   b. chi

   c. eta

   d. xi

4. Pick the name for the Greek letter σ:

   a. alpha

   b. omicron

   c. epsilon

   d. sigma

5. Which of these images represents the Greek letter omega?

6. Pick the English letter that corresponds to Greek letter γ:

   a. y

   b. i

   c. d

   d. g

7. Pick the Greek letter that corresponds to English letter-combination ps:

a. ψ

b. φ

c. ς

d. π

8. Pick the name for the Greek letter ω:

a. mu

b. omega

c. omicron

d. gamma

9. Which of these images represents the Greek letter delta?

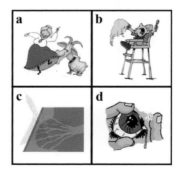

10. Pick the English letter that corresponds to Greek letter Ξ:

a. X

b. E

c. S

d. G

11. Pick the English letter that corresponds to Greek letter Δ:

    a. T

    b. D

    c. G

    d. A

12. Pick the English letter that corresponds to Greek letter ω:

    a. a

    b. w

    c. o

    d. v

13. For the following images, pick the Greek letter associated with them:

Ω ζ ξ Δ Λ χ

14. Which of these images represents the Greek letter xi?

15. Pick the name for the Greek letter ζ:

    a. xi

    b. beta

    c. zeta

    d. gamma

16. Pick the Greek letter that corresponds to English letter-combination ph:

    a. π

    b. ρ

    c. ψ

    d. φ

17. Pick the English letter that corresponds to Greek letter σ:

    a. o

    b. a

    c. s

    d. w

18. For the following images, pick the Greek letter associated with them:

    ς ω μ θ φ λ

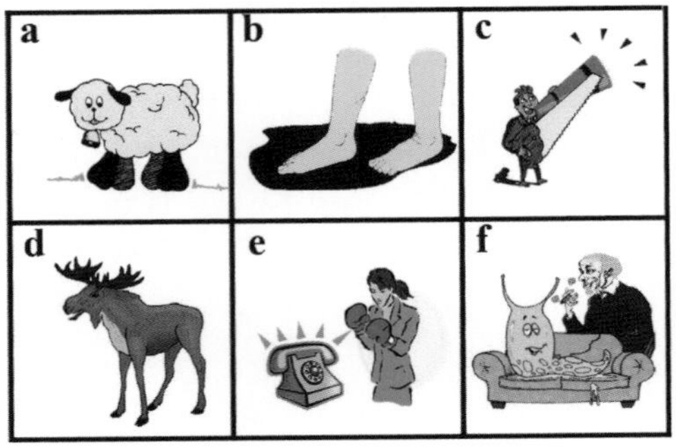

19. Pick the Greek letter that corresponds to English letter o:

    a. epsilon

    b. omega

    c. upsilon

    d. omicron

20. Pick the Greek letter that corresponds to English letter-combination ch / kh:

    a. χ

    b. φ

    c. H

    d. ξ

Vocabulary

List 1

ἐπώνυμος	ῥινόκερως
σῠνώνῠμος	μάσταξ
γυνή	γνάθος
ἀνδρόγυνος	ὀδούς
Ἀλέξανδρος	ἀριθμός
πατριώτης	μᾰστῐχάω
ἐγώ	γένυς
ἰδιώτης	ἀρθρῖτις
κέρας	μύσταξ

ἁρμόζω

κύλινδρος

ἁρμός

γόνυ

σκολίωσις

ποταμός

ἄριστος

List 2

ζῷον

πέτασος

ὀκτώπους

χορδή

πτερόω

ὀμφαλός

καρδιά

πλοῦτος

ἡπᾰτίζων

γενέτωρ

ζῳδῐᾱκός

λίπος

σπλήν

νεφρός

ὕπνος

ἄνεμος

σῠμπόσῐον

γένεσις

πτέρυξ

φυσικός

δεσπότης

πούς

γνωτός

Καλυψώ

ἀποκαλύπτω

List 3

γῆρας

Γραικός

ὀστέον

πτερωτός

βίος

ζωός

σκεπτῐκός

ἀμβροσία

νεκρός

αἰών

Ἡρακλῆς

Περικλῆς

κλίνω

γεραρός

γεραιός

κλῑμᾰκτηρῐκός

σὔνοψῑς

νέκυς

καλύπτω

ἀποκάλυψις

ὤψ

ὀπτικός

κλῖμαξ

ὀφθαλμός

ὄψις

List 4

οἶκος

χᾰρῐσμᾰ

ἴστωρ

γνῶσις

ἀγνωσῐᾱ

θεωρός

ἰδέᾱ

θεωρίᾱ

ἀμνησίᾱ

μάθημα

γνώμων

ἱστορίᾱ

θεώρημα

μᾰθημᾰτῐκός

Προμηθεύς

αὐτόματος

ἀνορεξία

δέρμα

χαίρω

οἰκέω

ὀρφανός

ἕδρᾱ

στάσις

ἱστορικός

χάρις

List 5

ἀγωνιστής

ἔκστᾰσῐς

βάσις

ναῦς

ἐξήγησις

ἡγεμών

στᾰτός

ἡγεμονῐᾱ

μεταφέρω

ἄνᾰβᾰσῐς

δημᾰγωγός

παιδᾰγωγός

ἀγωνία

σῠνᾰγωγή

δούξ

θέσις

ἀντίθεσις

παρένθεσις

στοᾱ́

κᾰτᾰβᾰσῐς

δόγμα

ἀποθεόω

ἐνθουσῐᾰσμός

σχίσις

βάλλω

List 6

λογῐστῐκός

βαλλίζω

σῠνθεσῐς

ὑπόθεσις

Θησεύς

ἔθος

ἠθικός

ναυτικός

ἠθολόγος

ἐθνικός

δόξᾰ

πᾰρᾰ́δοξος

ἄξων

δογματικός

θεός

ἀποθέωσις

ἔνθεος

ναύτης

ἐνθουσῖαστής   δημοκρᾱτῖᾱ
δῆμος   τύπος
ἔνδημος   γράμμα
σχιστός

List 7

δεξιτερός   δόσις
ἀγρός   λογῐσμός
ναυσία   στρατηγία
δαίμων   τυπικός
Νέμεσις   γρᾰμμή
ἄθεος   ἐνέργεια
ῠ̔πόκρῐσῐς   ὄργανον
σχίζω   παράδεισος
λόγος   σχῆμα
βόλος   τελέω
ὀβελίσκος   ἄρκτος
πᾰρᾰβᾰ́λλω   ῐ̔ππόδρομος
στρᾰτηγός

List 8

γραφεύς   τέκτων
δοτός   δέμω
καταγράφω   γραμματικός
πρόγραμμα   ἀρχιτέκτων

ἔργον γραπτός

γραφή ἱπποπότᾰμος

δημοκρᾱτῐκός Φίλῐππος

ῥάδιξ ταῦρος

ἀρκτικός ὄρνιθος

κῠνῐκός γράφω

ἵππος ἕλιξ

ἐνεργός γάλακτος

δόμος

List 9

γαλαξίας ἀτμός

ἀστήρ ὕδρα

Ζεύς δῐάρροιᾰ

ἥλιος ῥυθμός

πλαστῐκός ὅλος

Μέδουσᾰ ἑτερογενής

λύγξ ἀθλητής

φᾰντᾰσῐᾱ ἕξ

ᾱθλητῐκός ὀκτώ

Στέντωρ δέκα

λάκκος πρεσβῠτερος

ὕδωρ πρῶτος

φᾰντᾰσμᾰ

List 10

πρότερος

αὐθεντικός

ἄλλος

μέσος

βρᾰχῑ́ων

χολή

μᾱκρός

πρόμος

αὐτός

βαρύς

πλᾰτύς

δύο

μεσοποτάμιος

πλάσσω

μόνος

βυθός

ἄβυσσος

πλάσμᾰ

μεγᾰλος

νέος

γυμνάζω

χλωρός

πλάστης

αὐξάνω

θώρᾱξ

List 11

ἡδονή

πολιός

κῶνος

μέταλλον

πορφύρεος

μηχανή

ἥρως

θεράπων

μύστης

ἡρωίνη

γιγνώσκειν

διδάσκω

εὑρίσκειν

μηχανικός

ἔρως

φόβος

ψύχειν

ζῆλος

κάτοπτρον   λείπω
μύωψ   ἄκᾰνθᾰ
σκηνή   μεταλλικός
θεραπεύειν

List 12

δεινός   κόπρος
ὑγιής   σκέλος
κενός   σηπτικός
πρέσβυς   τύραννος
γλαυκός   ἄξιος
ωχρός   πυρετός
πτερίδος   ζώνη
κηρός   πρίσμα
στίγμα   σύριγξ
κῆτος   πόλος
βοῦς   στίζειν
σῆψις   σήπειν
μάρσιππος

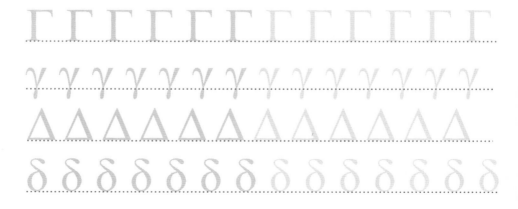

Quick practice

 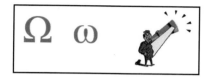

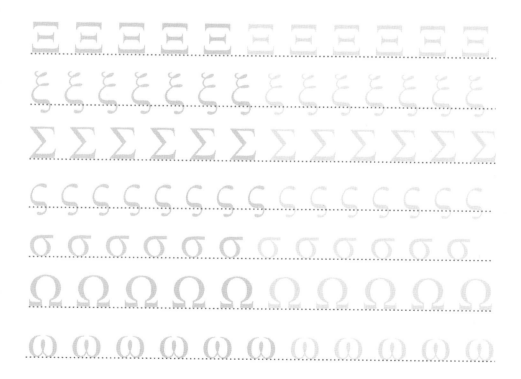

Learning the alphabet

Now that you know the letters, it's time to consolidate them into the alphabet, and learn their order — vital if you're to look words up in a dictionary, and also useful for cementing them into your long-term memory. This is partly because it gives you other connections and potential retrieval cues, and also because it will provide another way of practicing your letters.

Although we're learning them in alphabetical order, we won't try and grasp them right away as one long chain. Once again, we'll chunk them. Here are the first 8 letters with the English transliteration.

A	α	a	alpha
B	β	b	beta
Γ	γ	g	gamma
Δ	δ	d	delta
E	ε	e	epsilon
Z	ζ	z	zeta
H	η	e	eta
Θ	θ	th	theta

How to remember this order? You could try repeating the names over and over, while looking at the Greek letters. This is the default strategy of most students, and I mention it so I can clearly and explicitly say: this is not a good strategy!

A better step would be to write the Greek letters as you repeat the English transliterations, but this is still far from the best strategy (although writing the Greek letters is itself a good thing to do). No, this sort of situation — remembering the order of things — is exactly what list mnemonics were designed to help with.

List mnemonics are exactly what they sound like: mnemonic strategies for learning lists of ordered items. The famous mnemonic strategy variously called the Roman Room method, the journey method, the method of loci, is an example of this type of strategy. So is the pegword mnemonic, the link mnemonic, and the story (or sentence) mnemonic.

The particular list mnemonic that is most suited for this situation is the story mnemonic. Here, then, is a mnemonic story, with associated images, to help you learn the order of these first eight letters.

This image of the text is to re-emphasize the visual aspect from the cards, but here is the 'story' in a more readable format:

*the elf shares **beets** with Grandma but on the delta Pepsi revives the cheetah when his child won't eat the tar*

The **elf** shares **beets** with **Grandma** but on the **delta Pepsi** revives the **cheetah** when his child won't **eat the tar**.

Now I know, if you haven't used this sort of mnemonic before, it's going to seem silly to you, and you won't believe it's really going to help! But do try; I do assure you that this sort of strategy is of proven effectiveness. You really will be surprised how much easier such nonsensical stories are to remember than a list of words, or, worse, a list of letters. (If you want to come up with your own story based on these words, in this order, feel free! if you've created it yourself, it will probably work better.)

So what do you do with this story? Rather than repeating letters while picturing the Greek letters, repeat the story while visualizing the images. Yes, you still need some repetition, but you'll find you need far less than you would for less memorable information. Once you have the story firmly fixed in your head, visualize the Greek letters as you say each keyword.

When you're confident you've got this first story in your head, you can move on to the next 8 letters:

Here is their mnemonic story:

Keep your eye out for a cap for the lamb saying moo as the newborn skis home for pie

Keep your eye out for a **cap** for the **lamb** saying **moo** as the **newborn skis** home for **pie**.

I	ι	i	iota
K	κ	k	kappa
Λ	λ	l	lambda
M	μ	m	mu
N	ν	n	nu
Ξ	ξ	x	xi
O	o	o	omicron
Π	π	p	pi

The trick to mastering these stories is to really think about each link: the disembodied giant eye staring down at the graduate's cap, the lamb saying moo (thinking she's a cow?), the newborn baby laughing at that, swinging wildly in the hand of the skier, and so on. Pay particular attention to the weaker connections in the story, such as the cap for the lamb (you want to remember the cap comes first, so putting it on the lamb might be confusing), or the moo at the newborn. You can elaborate these if necessary, such as visualizing a pointy corner of the cap prodding the lamb's tail.

Once you've got that story fixed in your mind, remind yourself of the first set. When you're confident you've got both sets mastered, move on to the 3rd set of 8 letters:

and its mnemonic story:

Row, Sigmund! The tower is upside-long from the fight with the kite sent by the psychic with the megaphone

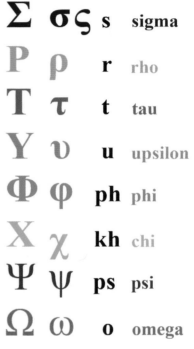

Σ	σ ς	s	sigma
Ρ	ρ	r	rho
Τ	τ	t	tau
Υ	υ	u	upsilon
Φ	φ	ph	phi
Χ	χ	kh	chi
Ψ	ψ	ps	psi
Ω	ω	o	omega

Row, Sigmund! The **tower** is **upside-long** from the **fight** with the **kite** sent by the **psychic** with the **megaphone**.

Once you've mastered the 3 mnemonic stories, you'll realize there's some other obvious weak connections — namely, those between each set. How do you remember which set follows which? Two brief phrases can help with this:

- Tar in my eye
- Pie for Sigmund

Here's the complete alphabet, all together:

A	α	alpha
B	β	beta
Γ	γ	gamma
Δ	δ	delta
E	ε	epsilon
Z	ζ	zeta
H	η	eta (long e)
Θ	θ	theta
I	ι	iota
K	κ	kappa
Λ	λ	lambda
M	μ	mu
N	ν	nu
Ξ	ξ	xi
O	ο	omicron
Π	π	pi
P	ρ	rho
Σ	σ ς	sigma
T	τ	tau
Y	υ	upsilon
Φ	φ	phi
X	χ	chi
Ψ	ψ	psi
Ω	ω	omega (long o)

Greek Roots (and Further Practice)

This final section has two purposes. The first is to provide both additional practice in recognizing the Greek letters, and more words to learn. The second is for those readers who are interested in extending their understanding of English, especially scientific, medical, and technical words. The words in this section all provide roots for English words — prefixes, suffixes, stems. Much of the vocabulary used in medicine, botany, and zoology, in particular, derives (ultimately or directly) from Greek words. A knowledge of these words can stand you in good stead when required to learn such academic terms, or give you a good starting point for understanding if confronted with them in your reading material.

I have sorted the words into groups based on meaning, to give greater meaningfulness (and aid memory). In this section, the Greek words are simply listed, to provide reading practice. The transliterations, meanings, and English descendants, appear in the Glossary. Note that this shouldn't be considered an authoritative source for Greek roots! I haven't distinguished between English words that derive directly from the Greek, and those that derive from Latin words that derive from the Greek. In a few cases, the Latin doesn't itself derive from the Greek, but both words descend from a common ancestor (Proto-Indo-European). In all cases, however (unless explicitly stated otherwise), the words are all cognate.

The list is also not comprehensive — I have selected only those with at least one English word in common usage.

And, of course, this list doesn't include all the words in this book that are useful roots! A number of the words in the foregoing lists could also be included there; they have merely been excluded because of their earlier appearance. However, some of the words in those lists, if they're connected to Greek words in the Roots lists, are mentioned as related.

In the Glossary section, you'll see the example English words include a wide range, from common to extremely technical. I am very aware that the words one knows are very idiosyncratic! What seems common to me may well be unknown to you; what I find obscure, you may well find to be very familiar. To use these lists to learn more Greek words, simply choose (and underline or highlight) one or two English words that are well-known to you, that you can use as hooks for memory. If you don't know any of the English words, feel free to omit that Greek word from remembering (but of course you can still use it for letter recognition!).

For those also interested in extending their English vocabulary, the variety of words is intended to show you the different ways the Greek root can appear, and to get you used to recognizing Greek-based words and dissecting them into their component parts. Notice that I have sprinkled the examples with notes of other Greek roots in the word, or explanations of the meaning of the English word. These are intended to stimulate your thinking. The listed examples would be very unwieldy if I was comprehensive with this, and in any case, it is far better for your learning to work out the connections yourself.

I have kept the category headings in these reading practice lists, to give you a head start in guessing the meanings of the words.

Note that in a very few cases, you'll see two variants of the word on the same line. The second will usually be the genitive case, and is there because the link to the English words is more obvious in that variant.

Directional

ἔνδον	πρόσθεν
εἰς	διά
ἔσω	παρά
ἐσωτερικός	σύν
ἐκτός	συμβάλλειν
ἔξω	συνάγειν
πρό	συστέλλειν
προβάλλειν	ἄκρος
πρός	

Comparative

ἕτερος	μέρος
ὁμός	πᾶς
ὅμοιος	τέλος
ἴσος	

Quality

ἀ- / ἀν-	στερεός
δυσ-	σκληρός
κᾰκός	τραχύς
κᾰκῐστος	εὐρύς
μῖσος	ἀνευρύνειν
εὖ	μέγας
καλός	μικρός
ὀρθός	κλαστός
στρεπτός	καυστός
ψευδής	γλυκύς
ἔτυμος	ὑγρός
ὀξύς	γυμνός
ταχύς	κρυπτός
σοφός	ξένος
μωρός	καινός
παχύς	παλαιός
βαθύς	γέρων

Number

δίς

δίχα

διπλόος

δεύτερος

ἄμφίς

ἥμισυς

τέτταρες

ὀλίγος

πολύς

οἱ πολλοί

μυρίος

Colour

λευκός

μέλας

κυάνεος

χρῡσός

χρῡσαλλίς

Biology

γένος

γόνος

ᾠόν

Plant

δένδρον

ξύλον

ὕλη

ἄνθος

ἄνθεμον

ῥόδον

κᾰρπός

μύκης

σάκχαρον

σῖτος

οἶνος

βλαστάνειν

φύω

φύσις

σπείρω

σπόρος

σπορᾱ́

σπέρμα

ζευγνύναι

ζῠγόν

ζυγωτός   κύτος
γάμος   ἀγγεῖον
γαμέτης   μυελός
κοινός   γλία
κοίνωσις   κόλλᾰ

Animal

κΰων   μίτος
ὄρνις   νῆμα
σαύρα   χόνδρος
ὄφις   μῦς
σάρξ   οὐρᾱ́
σῶμα   σκίουρος
στόμα   ὄνυξ
τρῆμα   ἕρπειν
τρηματώδης

Mineral

πέτρα   ἄνθραξ
λίθος   ἅλς
ἤλεκτρον   ἅλινος
χᾰλκός

Human

ἄνθρωπος   παρθένος
πίθηκος   ὄντος
παῖς, παιδός   ἴδιος
παιδείᾱ

Mind

μνήμη	φιλία
βίβλος	εὐφρασία
σῆμα	σώφρων
ποιεῖν	λᾰτρείᾱ
ποιητής	τᾰφος
ποίησις	ἐπιτάφιον
πράττειν	ἐπιτάφιος
πρᾶξις	θάνατος
πρᾶγμα	κλέπτειν
γλύφειν	κλέπτης
φίλος	πωλεῖν

Body

ἐγκέφᾰλος	ῠστέρᾱ
ῥίς, ῥινός	μήτρᾱ
βρόγχος	ὄρχις
γαστήρ	κύστις
χείρ	θάλαμος
δάκτυλος	φλέψ
μᾰστός	

Senses

αἴσθησῐς	δραστικός
αἰσθητικός	δρᾶμα
σκέπτεσθαι	μίμος
σκοποῦ	φᾰσῐς
δρᾶν	εἰκών

εἶδος

ὀσμή

οὖς

ὦτα

ἠχέω

ἠχώ

κατηχεῖν

φάναι

φημί

φήμη

φωνή

φθέγγεσθαι

φθόγγος

ἔπος

μῦθος

λέγειν

λέξῐς

λεξῐκός

λεξικόν

Digestion

ὀρέγειν

πέψις

πεπτός

φαγεῖν

Medical

ῑᾱτρός

ἄλγος

νόστος

ὀδύνη

πάθος

αἷμα

ἔμεσις

ἔμετος

σπεῖρα

ὄγκος

κρῑ́νω

ἐκκρίνειν

γλῶσσα

γλῶττα

Politics & Power

ἄρχω

δύναμις

κράτος

σθένος

στρατός

στρῶμα

τόξον
κρίσις
νέμω
νομός
νόμος
ἄνομος
κόσμος

κοσμεῖν
τάσσειν
τάξις
τάγμᾰ
ἔχω
ἕξῐς
στίχος

Gods

ἅγιος
ἱερός

δῖος

Places

πόλις
πολιτικός
τόπος
γῆ

νῆσος
πέλαγος
σπήλαιον
σπῆλυγξ

Physics

χρόνος

Light

οὐρανός
ἡμέρᾱ
σελήνη
φῶς, φωτός
φωσφόρος
ἀκτίς

χρῶμα
φλέγειν
φλέγμᾰ
φλόξ
θερμός

Shape

μορφή

γῦρος

κύκλος

σφαῖρα

ῥόμβος

λεπίς, λεπίδος

λεπτός

στῦλος

πόρος

ἀπορεῖν

ἄπορος

ὁδός

ὁδαῖος

Action

κινεῖν

κίνησις

κίνημα

χορεία

χορός

πλανᾶν

πλανήτης

ἄγω

ἡγέομαι

βαίνω

-βάτης

τρέχειν

τροχός

δρόμος

ἵστημι

στᾰτῐκός

στήλη

στρέφειν

στροφή

τρέπειν

τρόπου

φέρειν

φόρησις

διαφόρησις

διαφορεῖν

στέλλω

ἀπόστολος

ἐπιστέλλειν

λαμβάνειν

λῆψις

λῆμμα

τιθέναι

θησαυρός

θετός

θετῐκός

πίπτειν

πτῶσις

σύμπτωσις

ῥεῖν

ῥηγνύναι

τέμνειν

τόμος

ἔντομᾰ

ἐκτέμνειν

ἐκτομή

πλήσσειν

πλῆγμα

τύπτειν

πνεῖν

σφύζειν

σφυγμός

σφῠ́ξῐς

τείνειν

τετανός

τόνος

τᾰ́σῐς

ἐντείνειν

ἐκτείνω

ἔκτᾰσῐς

σπᾶν

σπᾰστῐκός

σπασμός

τρέφειν

κρᾶσῐς

λύειν

λύσις

ἀνάλυσις

σείειν

σεισμός

μείζων

πλαστός

Answers to review questions

Review 1.1

1. d
2. (a) I (b) E (c) B (d) O (e) A (f) T
3. c
4. d
5. d
6. d
7. (a) β (b) κ (c) τ (d) ε (e) ι (f) o
8. c
9. a
10. b

Review 1.2

1. b
2. c
3. c
4. b
5. b
6. a
7. c

8. d

9. d

10. c

11. b

12. c

13. c

14. a

15. d

Review 1.3

1. c

2. (a) H (b) M (c) Y (d) P (e) Z (f) A

3. d

4. b

5. d

6. b

7. (a) ι (b) E (c) N (d) μ (e) υ (f) X

8. d

9. d

10. a

11. c

12. (a) B (b) ζ (c) χ (d) K (e) T (f) ν

13. d

14. b

15. c

16. c

17. b

18. (a) η (b) ρ (c) I (d) α (e) ε (f) O

19. c

20. a

Review 1.4

1. (a) psi (b) phi (c) chi (d) pi (e) theta (f) lambda

2. d

3. c

4. d

5. b

6. (a) Θ (b) Υ (c) P (d) Φ (e) Ψ (f) Λ

7. a

8. d

9. a

10. (a) zeta (b) eta (c) theta (d) beta

11. c

12. a

13. c

14. (a) χ (b) η (c) N (d) κ (e) θ (f) M

15. c

Review 1.5

1. (a) δ (b) Σ (c) Ψ (d) Υ (e) γ (f) Ξ

2. c

3. d

4. d

5. c

6. d

7. a

8. b

9. c

10. a

11. b

12. c

13. (a) Δ (b) Λ (c) ξ (d) χ (e) Ω (f) ζ

14. c

15. c

16. d

17. c

18. (a) λ (b) θ (c) ω (d) μ (e) φ (f) ς

19. b, d

20. a

Glossary

Words chosen have been taken mostly from my Indo-European Cognate Dictionary, though many in the initial two lists are simply common words. With the exception of very short words found in the initial lists, words have been chosen either because of their close similarity to their English counterparts, or because their cognate relationship offers a hook for remembering ('cognate' means the Greek and English words ultimately have the same ancestor), or in some cases, because the word is common and a mnemonic is reasonably obvious.

Vocabulary for Group 1

αἰεί (aiei), always, ever, forever (Νῦν καὶ ἀεὶ. For ever and ever.) — cognate with aeon/eon, eternity, ever

ἐκ (ek), out of, from, since — cognate with the prefix ex-

εἴ (ei), you (sing.) are — cognate with *are*

καὶ (kai), and, also, too — cognate with co-, com-, con- meaning *with* (coagulate, collide, connect, etc)

κακοι (kakoi), bad, cowardly (pl.) — may be cognate with old word *cack*, meaning to defecate, and perhaps to cack-handed, also cacophony, kakistocracy

το (to), the — cognates (*the* comes in various forms, depending on whether the noun it's modifying is singular or plural, and what gender it is; the connection between its various forms and our *the* is not obvious but knowing they're cognates may help you pick out any similarities)

οἱ (oi), the (pl.) — cognates

ὅτι (oti), that — cognates

τί (ti), what?, why? — cognates (the connection to *why* is more obvious than *what*, and more obvious if you know the French *qui*) καιτοι (kaitoi), and yet — derived from και (kai) and τοι (toi), which provides emphasis in the meaning of *really, truly*

Vocabulary for Group 2

ἐν (en), in, on, at — cognates (note that when this is used as a prefix, it becomes εγ before γ, κ, χ)

το αἷμα (to aima), blood — hence haem- (haemoglobin, haemophilia, haemorrhage, etc), -emia (ischemia, leukemia, etc)

ὄνομᾰ (ónoma), name, noun — cognates

μέ (mé), me — cognates

ἐμέ (emé), me — cognates

ὄμμα (ómma), eye (poet.) — cognate with ophthalmology, optical, ocular

ἑκατόν (hekatón), hundred — cognates; hence hecato-, as in hecatomb

μιμέομαι (miméomai), I mimic — cognate with mimic and mime

ἄντα (ánta), over against, face to face — hence anta- (antagonist, antagonize, etc)

ὄζειν (ózein), to smell (exude a scent) — cognate with ozone

ἀντί (antí), over against, opposite, at the same time as, instead of — hence anti- (anticlockwise, antidote, antibiotic, etc)

εἶναι (einai), to be — cognate with essence, presence, interest, is

κατά (katá), down, against, back — as in catacombs, catabolic

ἀνά (aná), on, upon, up, up to — as in anagram, anabolic

μανίᾱ (maníā), madness, frenzy, enthusiasm — cognate with mania, maniac

ἀνομία (anomía), lawlessness — cognate with anomy, anomie

μετά (metá), among, over and above, concerning — as in metabolism, metamorphic, metaphor ἐννέα (ennéa), nine — cognates; hence ennead (set of 9 persons or things)

μεῖον (meîon), less, smaller — as in Miocene, meiosis

οἰκονομίᾱ (oikonomíā), economy, thrift — cognates

ἀμνίον (amníon), fetal membrane — hence amniotic and amniocentesis

μᾰντείᾱ (manteíā), prophecy, divination — hence geomancy, necromancy

Vocabulary for Group 3

List 1

ἀνήρ (anḗr), man, husband, human — cognate with andro- (androgynous, android), -ander (philander, Alexander), -andry (misandry, polyandry)

μήτηρ (mḗtēr), mother, source — cognate with maternal, maternity, mater

κρανίον (kraníon), skull — cognate with cranium, cranial

ἀρετή (aretḗ), goodness, virtue, character — cognate with harmony, order, rate, art

βᾰρεῖᾰ (bareîa), baria, the grave accent, indicating low pitch — cognate with baritone, barysphere, barometer

ἄρα (ára), so, then, therefore — cognate with order

χαρά (khará), joy — cognate with charisma; *cheer* is a good keyword

κῆρ (kêr), heart — cognate with core, cardiac, cardio- (cardiovascular, cardiogram, cardiologist)

ἁμαρτή (hamartḗ), at the same time, at once — cognate with harmony, order, rate, art

ἁρμονία (harmonía), joint, union — cognate with harmony, harmonious

βιοτή (biotḗ), from βίος (bíos), life — hence biota, biology, antibiotic, biography, biome, biopsy, biorhythm, symbiosis

νέκταρ (néktar), nectar — cognates

ὅραμα (hórama), a visible object, a spectacle — cognate with panorama ναυτία (nautía), nausea — cognates

χᾰρᾰκτήρ (kharaktḗr), instrument used for engraving, stamp, letter, characteristic — cognate with character, characteristic

τέχνη (tékhnē), craft, skill, art — cognate with technique, technology

ᾱ̓ήρ (āḗr), mist, air, wind — cognate with air, aero- (aeroplane, aerodynamics, aerobic, etc)

ὄρυζα (óruza), rice — cognate with rice, risotto, Oryza

βακτηρία (baktēría), rod, staff — hence bacteria (rod-shaped)

ἑκατόμβη (hekatómbē), sacrifice of a hundred oxen (from ἑκατόν, hundred + βοῦς, ox) — hence hecatomb (a great public sacrifice)

List 2

αὖ (aû), again, anew, further — cognate with auto- (automobile, autograph, autobiography, etc), though how a word meaning *again* birthed a word meaning *self* I'm not sure — perhaps through an alternative meaning of *the same*

βάκτρον (báktron), stick — cognate with peg; related to βακτηρία

μάμμη (mámmē), mamma, mother's breast — cognate with mammary, mammal, mama

ἄρτι (árti), this moment, just now — cognate with rate, order, art

κάρα (kára), head, face — cognate with cerebral, cerebrum, cranium, cornea, cheer

ὕαινα (húaina), hyena — cognates

χήρ (khḗr), hedgehog — hence echino- (echinoderm, echinology, etc); cognate with urchin

νεῦρον (neûron), sinew, cord, strength, nerve — hence neuron, nerve

ῥίζα (rhíza), root (plant), source, base — hence rhizome

χάρμα (khárma), source of joy — cognate with charisma; *charm* is a good keyword μήνη (mḗnē), moon — cognates, also cognate with menses, menstruation, menopause

ἀράχνη (arákhnē), spider, web — hence Arachne, arachnoid

μέτρον (métron), something used to measure, length, metre (poet.) — hence metre, meter

αὔρᾱ (aúrā), breeze, steam — cognate with aura, air

ῥεῦμα (rheûma), stream, flow — hence rheumatic, rheum; also cognate with stream, rhythm, diarrhoea, serum

αὖτε (aûte), again — see αὖ (aû)

ἡμι- (hēmi-), half — hence hemi- (hemisphere, hemiplegia, hemidemisemiquaver, etc)

τρι- (tri-), three, thrice — cognates; hence tri- (tripod, triangle, tricycle)

αὐτάρ (autár), but, moreover — related to αὖτε (aûte) and αὖ (aû); this variant is more readily connected with its meaning, if you focus on the *ut*

ἔντερον (énteron), guts, bag — cognate with in, interior, entrails

List 3

ἅρμα (hárma), chariot — cognate with harmony, order, rate, art; *car* might be a useful keyword

κέντρον (kéntron), spike, thorn, nail, stationary point of a pair of compasses, centre of a circle — cognate with centre

τὸ αὐτό = ταὐτο, the same — from auto-, meaning self, same

ζύμη (zúmē), leaven — hence enzyme, zymosis

νάρκη (nárkē), numbness, torpor — hence narcolepsy, narcotic

βοτάνη (botánē), grass, herb — hence botany, botanic

ἔμβρῦον (émbruon), young one, embryo, fetus — cognate with embryo

ἄημι (áēmi), I breathe, blow — related to ᾱήρ (āḗr)

τραῦμα (traûma), wound, hurt, damage — cognate with trauma

οὖρον (oûron), urine — cognates

Vocabulary for Group 4

List 1

ὑπέρ (hupér), over, above, across — hence hyper- (hyperbola, hyperlink, hyperbole)

ἀπό (apó), from, away from — hence ap- (e.g., aphelion) and apo- (apogee, apocryphal, apostate, etc)

ὀνομᾰτοποιίᾱ (onomatopoiíā), onomatopoeia — cognates

πατήρ (patḗr), father — hence pater, paternal, paternity, etc

φράτηρ (phrátēr), community member, kinsman, citizen — cognate with fraternal, fraternity, brother

φυή (phuḗ), growth — cognate with chlorophyll, -phyte (epiphyte, neophyte, phytoplankton)

θυγάτηρ (thugátēr), daughter — cognates

ἄρθρον (árthron), joint, limb, connecting word — hence arthropod, arthritis, arthroscopy, etc

πέταλον (pétalon), leaf, slice — cognate with petal

ψάλλειν (psállein), to twitch, twang, play (on a harp) — hence psalm

πλοῖον (ploîon), ship, boat — cognate with float

ἧπαρ (hêpar), liver — hence hepatic, hepatitis

πῖνον (pînon), πῑ́νω (pī́nō) I drink — cognate with potion, poison, imbibe, beer

φῦλον (phûlon), a set of people, gender, nation — hence phylum, phylogenetics, phylogenesis (history of evolution of the animal or plant)

κλίμα (klíma), region, slope — cognate with climax, climatic, climacteric

πολεμεῖν (polemeîn), to make war, fight — cognate with polemarch, polemic

πλευρά (pleurá), a rib, side — cognate with pleurisy, pleura

φύλλον (phúllon), leaf, foliage, plant — hence chlorophyll, phyllotaxis ποτήρῐον (potérion), cup — cognate with potion, poison, potable

κλίνη (klínē), bed, couch — cognate with recline, clinic

List 2

τῆλε (tête), far off — hence tele- (telegram, telegraph, telepathy, etc)

πέτομαι (pétomai), I fly, I rush — cognate with petal; related to feather

ἄνᾰφορᾱ́ (anaphorá), reference of a thing to a standard — hence anaphora (repetition of same word or phrase in several successive clauses; use of a word which refers to a preceding word or phrase); uses same ending as metaphor

φῡλή (phūlḗ), a union of individuals into a community — hence phylum, phylogenetics, phylogenesis

ἄποθήκη (apothḗkē), repository, storehouse — cognate with apothecary, boutique

βῐβλῐοθήκη (bibliothḗkē), bookcase, library — cognate with French bibliothèque, biblio- (bibliophile, bibliography, bibliomania, etc), bible

θέμα (théma), that which is laid down, pile, horoscope, theme — cognates

ἠθολογῐᾱ (ēthologíā), a painting of character — cognate with ethology (study of character formation, study of animal behaviour)

θεοκρᾰτῐᾱ (theokratíā), theocracy — cognates

μύλη (múlē), mill — cognate with mill, molar, meal

πρόβλημᾰ (próblēma), obstacle, defense, problem — cognates

τῠ́μπᾰνον (túmpanon), drum, drumstick, wheel — cognate with tympani / timpani

θύρα (thúra), door, entrance — cognate with door, forum, thyroid

πετάννῡμι (petánnūmi), I spread out, open — cognate with petal

θηρῐον (thēríon), wild animal, beast — related to θήρ; cognate with feral, ferocious

φήρ (phḗr), alternative form of θήρ — cognate with feral

βουλῑμία (boulīmía), ravenous hunger — hence bulimia

Πάν (Pán) — cognate with Pan, panic

χίλιοι (khílioi), thousand — hence kilo, kilometre, kilogram

κεφαλή (kephalḗ), head, topmost part, most important part — hence cephalopod, hydrocephalus, microcephaly

List 3

λίνον (línon), anything made of flax — cognate with linen

θήρ (thḗr), wild beast, animal — hence thero-, therio- (e.g., theropod, theriomorphic), -there (used chiefly in the names of extinct mammals); cognate with feral, fierce

πρωΐ (prōḯ), early in the day — cognate with prior, proto- (Protozoa, prototype, proton, etc)

ὑπό (hupó), under, beneath — hence hypo- (hypodermic, hypocaust, hypothermia, etc)

τέφρα (téphra), ashes — cognate with tephra (ash ejected in a volcanic eruption), fever

πτερόν (pterón), feather, wing — cognate with pterodactyl, helicopter

φαινόμενον (phainómenon), that which is revealed, brought to light — cognate with phenomenon

παραβολή (parabolḗ), juxtaposition, comparison, parable — cognate with parable

ἆθλον (âthlon), prize, contest — cognate with athlete, athletics, pentathlon

πέντε (pénte), five — cognate with penta- (pentagon, pentagram, pentatonic, pentathlon, etc)

μᾰκροθῡμῐᾱ (makrothūmíā), patience — from macro- (macroeconomics etc) and -thymia (dysthymia, hyperthymia, etc), 'long temper'

πομπή (pompḗ), a sending, a solemn procession, pomp — cognate with pomp, psychopomp

αἰθήρ (aithḗr), heaven, aether — cognate with aether, ether, ethereal

πῦρ (pûr), a fire, lightning — hence pyrotechnics, pyromania, pyre φορά (phorá), carrying, bearing — hence metaphor, pheromone

πέρᾱ (pérā), beyond — cognate with peri- (perimeter, periscope, periphery, etc); a good keyword to distinguish from similar others would be *peer beyond*

φυτόν (phutón), plant, tree, creature, child — hence neophyte, phytoplankton

πέρᾱν (pérān), across, opposite — cognate with peri- (perimeter, periscope, periphery, etc); a good keyword to distinguish from similar others would be *ran across*

ψυχή (psukhḗ), life, soul, ghost, mind, spirit — hence psychology, psychic, psyche

θηλή (thēlḗ), teat, nipple, head of a pole — used in endothelium, epithelium, mesothelium

List 4

τράπεζα (trápeza), a table — cognate with trapezium, trapeze (probably because originally the ropes formed a trapezium with roof and cross-bar)

πάλιν (pálin), back, backwards, again, once more — hence palindrome

λᾰλῐᾱ́ (laliā́), talking, talk — hence -lalia used to denote speech disorders, e.g., echolalia

ἐποχή (epokhḗ), check, cessation, pause, epoch of a star (the point at which it seems to stop after reaching the highest) — cognate with epoch (which also has the meaning of a fixed point in time, as well as the more common sense of a period of time)

φάρμακον (phármakon), drug, medicine, potion — hence pharmacy, pharmacology

ἑπτά (heptá), seven — hence hepta- (heptagon, heptameter, Heptateuch)

περί (perí), about, concerning, around — cognate with peri- (perimeter, periscope, periphery, etc)

θέατρον (théatron), theatre, gathering place, spectacle — cognate with amphitheatre, theatre / theater, theatrical

πρίν (prín), before — cognate with prior

φρήν (phrḗn), midriff, heart, wits, mind, will — cognate with schizophrenia, frenetic

πιέζειν (piézein), to squeeze, repress — hence piezoelectric, piezometer

πνεῦμα (pneûma), air, wind, breath, life, spirit — hence pneumatic, pneumonia

ποίημα (poíēma), a work, creation, poem — cognate with poem, poetic

πτυχή (ptukhḗ), a fold — hence triptych, diptych

θαῦμα (thauma), wonder, marvel — hence thaumatrope, thaumaturge; *dream* might be a good keyword

πύλη (púlē), gate, door, entrance — hence pylon, Thermopylae, pylorus

θέρμη (thérmē), heat— hence thermos, thermal, hypothermia, thermometer

τροφή (trophḗ), nourishment, food, upbringing — cognate with trophic, phototrophic, atrophy, dystrophy

πέπερι (péperi), pepper — cognates

πόρνη (pórnē), female prostitute — hence pornography

Vocabulary for Group 5

List 1

ἐπώνυμος (epṓnumos), named in a significant manner — cognate with eponymous

σὺνώνῠμος (sunṓnumos), having the same name, having the only one meaning — cognate with synonymous

γυνή (gunḗ), woman, female, wife — cognate with gynaecological, misogyny

ἀνδρόγυνος (andrógunos), hermaphrodite, man who is effeminate — cognate with androgynous

Ἀλέξανδρος (Aléxandros) — cognate with Alexander

πατριώτης (patriṓtēs), fellow countryman — cognate with patriot

ἐγώ (egṓ), I — cognate with ego, egoist, egotistical

ἰδιώτης (idiṓtēs), private person, commoner, ignorant person, idiot — cognate with idiot

κέρας (kéras), horn — cognates; also cognate with keratin, rhinoceros

ῥινόκερως (rhinókerōs), rhinoceros — cognates

μάσταξ (mástax), jaws, what chews — cognate with masticate; *mastiff* would be a good keyword

γνάθος (gnáthos), jaw, narrow strait, edge — cognate with agnathous, gnathic, prognathic, prosognathous

ὀδούς (odoús) / ὀδών (odṓns), tooth, tusk — cognate with orthodontist, periodontal, mastodon

ἀριθμός (arithmós), number, amount, arithmetic — cognate with arithmetic, logarithm

μᾰστῐχᾰ́ω (mastikháō), I grind the teeth — cognate with masticate

γένυς (génus), jaw, mouth — cognate with chin

ἀρθρῖτις (arthrîtis), of or in the joint — cognate with arthritis

μύσταξ (mústax), upper lip — cognate with moustache

ἁρμόζω (harmózō), to fit together, join, betroth, govern — cognate with harmony, harmonious

κύλινδρος (kúlindros), round stone, marble, cylinder, roll of a book — cognate with cylinder

ἁρμός (harmós), joint, link — cognate with arm, harmony

γόνυ (gónu), knee — cognates; also cognate with genuflect, -agon (hexagon, pentagon, octagon, etc), trigonometry

σκολίωσις (skolíōsis), bending — cognate with scoliosis, colon

ποταμός (potamós), river — hence Potomac River, Mesopotamia ("the land between the rivers"), hippopotamus (river horse)

ἄριστος (áristos), best, bravest, noblest — cognate with aristocrat

List 2

ζῷον (zōîon), animal, beast, image — related to ζωός (zōós); cognate with zoo, zoology, -zoa (e.g., Protozoa), -zoic (e.g., Mesozoic)

πέτασος (pétasos), broad-brimmed hat, broad leaf, awning — cognate with petal

ὀκτώπους (oktṓpous), eight-footed, octopus — cognates

χορδή (khordḗ), guts, string, chord — cognate with chord, cord

πτερόω (pteróō), to feather — cognate with pterodactyl, helicopter

ὀμφαλός (omphalós), navel, centre — cognate with omphalic, umbilical, navel

καρδιά (kardiá), heart, mind, stomach — hence cardiac, cardio-
(cardiovascular, cardiogram, cardiologist)

πλοῦτος (ploûtos), wealth — hence plutocracy, plutocrat

ἡπᾰτίζων (hēpatízōn), liver-coloured — hence hepatic, hepatitis

γενέτωρ (genétōr), ancestor, father, author — cognate with progenitor, genesis, genetic

ζῳδῐᾰκός (zōidiakós), of or relating to little animals; of or relating to the zodiac — cognates (think of the zodiac as a parade of little animals)

λίπος (lípos), fat, oil — hence lipo- (e.g., liposuction), lipids

σπλήν (splḗn), spleen — cognates

νεφρός (nephrós), kidney, mind — hence nephrology, nephritis

ὕπνος (húpnos), sleep, death — hence hypno- (hypnotherapy, hypnosis, hypnotist, hypnagogic)

ἄνεμος (ánemos), wind, breeze — hence anemometer, anemone
(windflower)

σὖμπόσῐον (sumpósion), drinking party, feast, party, symposium —
cognate with symposium

γένεσις (génesis), origin, creation — cognate with genesis, genetic

πτέρυξ (ptérux), wing — cognate with pterodactyl, helicopter, feather φυσικός (phusikós), natural, native, physical — cognate with physical, physics

δεσπότης (despótēs), master, lord, despot — cognate with despot

πούς (poús), foot, leg — cognate with tripod, podiatry

γνωτός (gnōtós), known — from γνῶσις, knowledge; cognate with agnostic, gnosis

Καλυψώ (Kalupsṓ), Calypso

ἀποκαλύπτω (apokalúptō), I reveal — cognate with apocalypse

List 3

γῆρας (gêras), old age — hence geriatric, gerontology, progeria

Γραικός (Graikós), Greek — cognates

ὀστέον (ostéon), bone, rock — hence osteo- (osteoarthritis, osteology, osteopathy)

πτερωτός (pterōtós), winged — cognate with pterodactyl, helicopter, feather

βίος (bíos), life — hence biology, biography, biopsy, symbiosis

ζωός (zōós), alive, living — hence zoology, -zoa (e.g., protozoa), -zoic (e.g., Mesozoic), zooid, zoo

σκεπτῐκός (skeptikós), thoughtful, inquiring — cognate with sceptical, sceptic

ἀμβροσία (ambrosía), ambrosia — cognates

νεκρός (nekrós), dead — hence necro- (necropolis, necromancer, necrosis, necrotic, necrophilia)

αἰών (aiōn), lifetime, generation, eon, eternity — cognate with aeon/eon

Ἡρακλῆς (Hēraklês), Heracles

Περικλῆς (Periklês), Pericles

κλίνω (klínō), to bend, slant, decline — cognate with decline, recline γεραρός (gerarós), stately, majestic; reverend — cognate with geriatric

γεραιός (geraiós), old, aged; old man — cognate with geriatric

κλῑμᾰκτηρῐκός (klīmaktērikós), climacteric — cognates

σύνοψῑς (súnopsis), a seeing all together, shared view, epitome, recapitulation — cognate with synopsis

νέκυς (nékus), corpse — related to νεκρός

καλύπτω (kalúptō), to cover, conceal — cognate with apocalypse, calypso, occult, conceal, cellar

ἀποκάλυψις (apokálupsis), revelation — cognate with apocalypse

ὤψ (ṓps), to the eye — cognate with optics, optical, optician

ὀπτικός (optikós), relating to vision — cognate with optical, optics

κλῖμαξ (klîmax), ladder, staircase, climax (rhetorical) — cognate with climax

ὀφθαλμός (ophthalmós), eye, sight, understanding — hence ophthalmology

ὄψις (ópsis), view — cognate with optics, optical, optician

List 4

οἶκος (oîkos), house, estate — cognate with eco- (economy, economics, ecology)

χάρῐσμᾰ (khárisma), grace, favor, gift — cognate with charisma

ἵστωρ (hístōr), judge, witness, wise man — cognate with history

γνῶσις (gnôsis), inquiry, knowledge, fame — cognate with agnostic, gnosis, -gnomy (e.g., physiognomy)

ἀγνωσῐ́ᾱ (agnōsíā), ignorance, obscurity — cognate with agnosia, agnostic

θεωρός (theōrós), spectator, envoy sent to an oracle — cognate with theory (see θεωρίᾱ) ἰδέᾱ (idéā), appearance, form, type, style — cognate with idea, ideo-

θεωρίᾱ (theōríā), embassy, spectacle, theory — cognate with theory (think of this in its meaning of something to contemplate, speculate about)

ἀμνησία (amnēsía), forgetfulness — cognate with amnesia

μάθημα (máthēma), lesson, learning, knowledge, the mathematical sciences, astrology — cognate with mathematics

γνώμων (gnṓmōn), interpreter, sundial — cognate with gnomon

ἱστορία (historía), inquiry, examination, body of knowledge, written account of such inquiries — cognate with history, story

θεώρημα (theṓrēma), speculation, proposition to be proved — cognate with theorem

μᾰθημᾰτῐκός (mathēmatikós), mathematical, mathematics — cognates

Προμηθεύς (Promētheús), Prometheus

αὐτόματος (autómatos), self-willed, unbidden, self-moving, growing wild — cognate with automaton, automatic

ἀνορεξία (anorexía), without appetite — hence anorexia

δέρμα (dérma), skin, hide — cognate with dermis, epidermis, dermatology, taxidermy, hypodermic (because it goes under the skin)

χαίρω (khaírō), to be full of cheer, to enjoy — related to χαρά; cognate with charisma; *cheer* is a good keyword

οἰκέω (oikéō), I inhabit, colonize, govern — cognate with eco- (economy, economics, ecology), ecumenical (belonging to the whole world)

ὀρφανός (orphanós), orphaned, childless, bereft — cognates

ἕδρᾱ (hédra), seat, chair, sitting, face of a regular solid — hence polyhedron, dodecahedron; cognate with cathedra (chair or seat of a bishop)

στάσις (stásis), standing stone, building, stature, position — cognate with static, stasis, stance, stand, status, stature, statue

ἱστορικός (historikós), exact, scientific, pertaining to history — cognate with historic, historical

χάρις (kháris), beauty, grace, gratitude — cognate with charisma

List 5

ἀγωνιστής (agōnistḗs), combatant, contestant, actor, champion — cognate with protagonist, antagonize, agony, agonize

ἔκστᾰσῐς (ékstasis), displacement from proper place, astonishment, trance — cognate with ecstasy

βάσις (básis), step, rhythm, foot, foundation — cognate with basis, base

ναῦς (naûs), ship — cognate with nautical, nausea

ἐξήγησις (exḗgēsis), narration, interpretation — cognate with exegesis (interpretation of a text)

ἡγεμών (hēgemṓn), one who goes first, guide, leader, governor — cognate with hegemon, hegemony

στᾰτός (statós), standing — cognate with static, stasis, stance, stand, status

ἡγεμονῐ́ᾱ (hēgemoníā), leadership, command; supremacy — cognate with hegemony

μεταφέρω (metaphérō), to carry over, transfer, change — cognate with metaphor

ἀνᾰ́βᾰσῐς (anábasis), ascent — cognate with anabasis (going up, a military advance); derives from βάσις and ἀνά-

δημᾰγωγός (dēmagōgós), popular leader, demagogue — cognates

παιδᾰγωγός (paidagōgós), teacher, guide — cognate with pedagogue, pedagogical

ἀγωνία (agōnía), contest, struggle for victory, agony — cognate with agony

σῠνᾰγωγή (sunagōgḗ), gathering, meeting, place of such assembly — cognate with synagogue

δούξ (doúx), leader — cognate with dux, ducal, duke

θέσις (thésis), arrangement, deposit, adoption, conclusion, thesis — cognates

ἀντίθεσις (antíthesis), opposition, contradiction, antithesis — cognates παρένθεσις (parénthesis), insertion, parenthesis — cognates

στοά (stoá), portico, stoa — cognates

κᾰτᾰβᾰσῐς (katábasis), descent — cognate with katabasis (going down, a military retreat); derives from βάσις and κατα meaning *down*

δόγμα (dógma), opinion, belief, decision — cognate with dogma, dogmatic

ἀποθεόω (apotheóō), I deify — cognate with apotheosize (to deify; to glorify), apotheosis

ἐνθουσῐᾰσμός (enthousiasmós), inspiration, enthusiasm — cognates

σχίσις (skhísis), division, parting — cognate with schism

βάλλω (bállō), I throw, let fall, strike, tumble — cognate with ball, parabola, hyperbola, ballistic

List 6

λογῐστῐκός (logistikós), skilled in calculating, in reasoning — derived from λόγος; cognate with logistics

βαλλίζω (ballízō), to dance, jump about — derived from βάλλω; but *ballet* and *ball* (i.e., a social event where there's dancing) are good keywords

σῠνθεσῐς (súnthesis), composition, synthesis, agreement — cognates

ὑπόθεσις (hupóthesis), proposal, suggestion, purpose — cognate with hypothesis

Θησεύς (Thēseús), Theseus

ἔθος (éthos), habit, custom, disposition — cognate with ethos, ethology

ἠθικός (ēthikós), moral, expressing character — cognate with ethics, ethical

ναυτικός (nautikós), of or for a ship, naval, seafaring — cognate with nautical

ἠθολόγος (ēthológos), painting of character especially by mimic gestures — cognate with ethology (study of human and animal behaviour) ἐθνικός (ethnikós), national — cognate with ethnic, ethnicity

δόξᾰ (dóxa), expectation, opinion, glory — hence orthodox, orthodoxy, paradox, paradoxical

πᾰρᾰδοξος (parádoxos), contrary to expectation, strange — cognate with paradox

ἄξων (áxōn), axle, axis — cognates

δογματικός (dogmatikós), dogmatic — cognates

θεός (theós), deity, divine — cognate with theology, theocracy, theism

ἀποθέωσις (apothéōsis), apotheosis — cognates

ἔνθεος (éntheos), possessed by a god — cognate with enthused, enthusiasm

ναύτης (naútēs), sailor — cognate with nautical, astronaut, cosmonaut

ἐνθουσῐᾰστής (enthousiastḗs), enthusiast — cognates

δῆμος (dêmos), district, country, common people — hence democracy, demagogue, demographic, endemic

ἔνδημος (éndēmos), among one's people, native, endemic — cognates

σχιστός (skhistós), cloven, divided — see σχίζω; cognate with schizoid

δημοκρᾰτῐᾱ (dēmokratíā), democracy, popular government — cognates

τύπος (túpos), blow, mark, impression, type, pattern — cognate with type

γράμμα (grámma), that which is written / drawn, picture, letter, book — see γράφω; cognate with telegram

List 7

δεξιτερός (dexiterós), right hand — cognate with dexterous, dexterity

ἀγρός (agrós), field, land — cognate with agronomy, agriculture, acre

ναυσία (nausía), nausea — cognates

δαίμων (daímōn), god, goddess, departed soul, demon — cognate with daimon, demon, demonic

Νέμεσις (Némesis), Nemesis — hence nemesis

ἄθεος (átheos), without gods, godless — cognate with atheist

ὑπόκρῐσῐς (hupókrisis), answer, elocution, pretense, hypocrisy — cognate with hypocrisy

σχίζω (skhízō), I split, cleave, divide — hence schizophrenia, schizoid, schism

λόγος (lógos), word, story, reason, explanation — hence -logy (psychology, geology, biology, apology, trilogy, etc), -logue (dialogue, monologue), logic

βόλος (bólos), a throw with a net, a cast of dice — derived from βάλλω; but *bolas* is a good keyword if you're familiar with the throwing weapon

ὀβελίσκος (obelískos), small spit, skewer, anything shaped like a spit — cognate with obelisk

πᾰρᾰβᾰ́λλω (parabállō), I set side by side — derived from βάλλω + πᾰρᾰ- meaning *beside, near*; hence parable, parabola, paradox, parallel

στρᾰτηγός (stratēgós), army commander, general — cognate with strategy, strategic

δόσις (dósis), gift, permission, dose of medicine — cognate with dose, antidote

λογῐσμός (logismós), calculation, argument, thought — derived from λόγος; cognate with logistics, logic, -logism (neologism, syllogism)

στρατηγία (stratēgía), office of general, campaign — cognate with strategy, strategic

τυπικός (tupikós), impressionable, conforming to a type — cognate with typical

γρᾰμμή (grammḗ), stroke or line of a pen, outline, edge — see γράφω; note similarity to γράμμα

ἐνέργεια (enérgeia), activity, vigour, workmanship, cosmic force — cognate with energy

ὄργανον (órganon), instrument, tool, sense organ, musical instrument — cognate with organ

παράδεισος (parádeisos), garden, paradise — cognates

σχῆμα (skhêma), form, shape, appearance, manner, character, plan, scheme — cognate with scheme, schema, schematic

τελέω (teléō), to bring about, complete, perform, pay, belong to a class, consecrate — cognate with toll (payment, tax) and talisman (from τέλεσμᾰ, payment, but later a consecrated object); also ultimately cognate with tele-, as in telegram, telephone, television, telescope, etc

ἄρκτος (árktos), bear, the north — cognate with Arcturus, Arthur, Arctic, Antarctic (anti-Arctic)

ἵππόδρομος (hippódromos), hippodrome (circuit for chariot-racing) — cognates

List 8

γραφεύς (grapheús), painter, secretary, writer, scribe — see γράφω; cognate with graphical, graphic

δοτός (dotós), given — cognate with dose, donate, data, donor

καταγράφω (katagráphō), scratch, write down, draw in outline — see γράφω + κατα (down)

πρόγραμμα (prógramma), a written public notice, an edict — cognate with programme / program; see γράφω

τέκτων (téktōn), carpenter, builder, craftsman, author — hence ἀρχιτέκτων; cognate with architect, technique, technology, text, texture

δέμω (démō), to build, make — cognate with timber, dome, domestic, domesticate

γραμματικός (grammatikós), knowing one's letters, grammar — cognate with grammar, grammatical; see γράφω

ἀρχιτέκτων (arkhitéktōn), master builder, architect — cognates

ἔργον (érgon), deed, action, work, task — hence ergonomic, ergocentric (focused on work), ergometer (a device that measures work done by muscles), ergophobia (an irrational fear of work), etc

γραφή (graphḗ), drawing, painting, writing, description — cognate with graph; see γράφω δημοκρᾰτῐκός (dēmokratikós), democratic — cognates

ῥάδιξ (rhádix), branch, palm frond — descends from ῥίζα (root); cognate with radical, eradicate, radish

ἀρκτικός (arktikós), Arctic — cognates; derived from ἄρκτος

κῠνῐκός (kunikós), dog-like, churlish — cognate with cynic, cynical (the original Cynics were nicknamed κῠ́ωνες, dogs; they were supposedly quite uncouth)

ἵππος (híppos), horse — hence hippopotamus (river horse), hippodrome, hippomania, hippophilia, hippophobia, hippotherapy

ἐνεργός (energós), at work, active — cognate with energy, energetic

δόμος (dómos), house, household — hence domestic

γραπτός (graptós), painted, written — cognate with graphite; see γράφω

ἵπποπότᾰμος (hippopótamos), hippopotamus — cognates

Φῐ́λῐππος (Phílippos) name meaning fond of horses — cognate with Philip

ταῦρος (taûros), bull — hence Taurus, taurine (bull-like)

ὄρνιθος (órnithos), of a bird, chicken — hence ornithology

γράφω (gráphō), to scratch, cut into, draw, write — cognate with graph, graphic, -graph (autograph, telegraph, polygraph, photograph, paragraph, etc), grapheme, graft, -gram (telegram, hologram, program, etc), carve

ἕλιξ (hélix), anything twisted, winding, spiral — cognate with helix, helical, helicopter

γάλακτος (gálaktos), of milk, of the Milky Way galaxy — galactic, lactose, galactorrhoea (excessive production of milk), galactose (the sugar in milk)

List 9

γαλαξίας (galaxías), Milky Way galaxy — cognate with galaxy

ἀστήρ (astér), celestial body, illustrious person, starfish — cognate with astral, astronomy, astrology

Ζεύς (Zeús), Zeus

ἥλιος (hḗlios), sun, east, day — cognate with the sun-god Helios, heliotrope (because they're attracted to the sun), heliocentric, aphelion

πλαστῐκός (plastikós), fit for moulding, plastic — cognates

Μέδουσᾰ (Médousa), Medusa

λύγξ (lúnx), lynx — cognates

φᾰντᾰσῐ́ᾱ (phantasíā), appearance, display, pomp, impression, image — cognate with fantasy

ᾱ̓θλητῐκός (āthlētikós), athletic — cognates

Στέντωρ (Sténtōr), Stentor — hence stentorian

λάκκος (lákkos), pond for water-fowl, cistern, reservoir — cognate with loch, lagoon; *lake* is not actually cognate but is certainly a good keyword

ὕδωρ (húdōr), water, rain, sweat — hence hydrology, hydrogen, dehydrate, hydroponic, hydraulics

φᾰ́ντᾰσμᾰ (phántasma), phantom, ghost, vision, fantasy — cognate with phantom, fantasy, phantasm

ἀτμός (atmós), steam, smoke — cognates with atmosphere

ὕδρα (húdra), sea serpent, hydra — cognate (note similarity to hydro-, meaning pertaining to water)

δῐᾱ́ρροιᾰ (diárrhoia), flowing through, diarrhoea — cognates

ῥυθμός (rhuthmós), rhythm, vibration, measure, proportion — cognates

ὅλος (hólos), whole, complete, generally — cognate with whole, hologram (each bit of a hologram contains information about the whole)

ἑτερογενής (heterogenḗs), heterogenous, of different kinds — cognates

ἀθλητής (athlētḗs), combatant, champion — cognate with athlete

ἕξ (héx), six — cognates; hence hexagon, hexameter, hexapod

ὀκτώ (oktṓ), eight — cognates; hence octopus, octagon

δέκα (déka), ten — cognates; hence decade, decimal

πρεσβῠ́τερος (presbúteros), older of two people, senior — cognate with presbyter (a Church elder), Presbyterian πρῶτος (prôtos), first, earliest, foremost — hence proton, protagonist, protein, protist, protocol, prototype, Protozoa

List 10

πρότερος (próteros), before, former, superior — hence Proterozoic

αὐθεντικός (authentikós), authentic, authoritative — cognates

ἄλλος (állos), other, another, different, else — hence allergy, allegory, allocentric, allogamy, allograph (written by someone other than the person concerned); also cognate with *alter*

μέσος (mésos), middle of, between, half, moderate — hence Mesolithic, Mesozoic

βρᾰχῑων (brakhī́ōn), upper arm, shoulder — cognate with brachial (belonging to the arm), brachiate (having arms; to move using arms); *branch* is a good keyword

χολή (kholḗ), gall, bile, wrath, disgust — cognate with choler, choleric, cholera

μᾰκρός (makrós), long, tall, deep, distant — hence macro- (macrobiotic, macrocosm, macroeconomics, macron)

πρόμος (prómos), foremost, leader, prince, champion — cognate with prime (think of prime minister), primary, primogeniture

αὐτός (autós), self, same — hence autograph, autonomy, automatic, automaton, autocracy, authentic, autism

βαρύς (barús), heavy, oppressive, deep, hollow — hence barometer, baritone, bariatric, hyperbaric, isobar

πλᾰτύς (platús), broad, flat — cognate with plate (think of the river plate, as well as metals), plateau, platypus (for its flat tail)

δύο (dúo), two — cognates; hence dual, duo

μεσοποτάμιος (mesopotámios), between two rivers — hence Mesopotamia

πλάσσω (plássō), I form, mould, imagine — cognate with plastic, plaster μόνος (mónos), alone, only, unique — hence monarch, monad, monastery, monastic, monk, monopoly, monotone

βυθός (buthós), depth, deep water — deep and depth may be cognates; *bottom* is a good keyword

ἄβυσσος (ábussos), bottomless, boundless, unfathomable — cognate with abyss, abyssal

πλάσμᾰ (plásma), something formed, figure, forgery, figment — cognate with plasma, plastic

μεγᾰ́λος (megálos), big, great, mighty — hence mega- (megalith, megalomania, megaphone, megalopolis)

νέος (néos), young, new — hence neonate, neologism, neophyte, neon, Neolithic; cognate with new

γυμνάζω (gumnázō), train, exercise, accustom — cognate with gymnast, gymnasium

χλωρός (khlōrós), green-yellow, pale, unripe, youthful — cognate with chlorine, chlorophyll, yellow, gold

πλάστης (plástēs), moulder, modeller, sculptor — cognate with plaster, plastic

αὐξάνω (auxánō), to make grow, increase — hence auxin (growth hormone); also cognate with auxiliary, augment, auction

θώρᾱξ (thṓrāx), corslet, coat of mail — cognate with thorax, thoracic

List 11

ἡδονή (hēdonḗ), delight, pleasure — cognate with hedonism, hedonist

πολιός (poliós), grey, grizzled — cognate with poliomyelitis (polio)

κῶνος (kônos), pine cone, pine tree, cone — cognate with cone, conic, conocarp

μέταλλον (métallon), mine, quarry, metal — cognate with metal, metallurgy

πορφύρεος (porphureos), purple — cognate with porphyria, porphyry μηχανή (mēkhanḗ), device, machine — cognate with machine, mechanism

ἥρως (hḗrōs), hero of Trojan War, demigod or human whose shrine is celebrated — cognate with hero

θεράπων (therápōn), attendant, aide, servant — cognate with therapist, therapy

μύστης (mústēs), initiate (one who has been initiated) — cognate with mysterious, mystery, mystic, mystical

ἡρωίνη (hērōínē), heroine, deceased woman — cognate with heroine

γιγνώσκειν (gignṓskein), to be aware of, perceive, observe, know — cognate with diagnostic, prognosis; see γνῶσις

διδάσκω (didáskō), I teach, instruct, train — cognate with autodidact, didactic

εὑρίσκειν (heurískein), to find out, find, fetch — cognate with eureka, heuristic

μηχανικός (mēkhanikós), ingenious, mechanical — cognate with mechanical

ἔρως (érōs), love, desire, passionate joy — cognate with erogenous, erotic, erotica, Eros

φόβος (phóbos), fear, panic, awe — cognate with phobia, phobic

ψύχειν (psúkhein), to breathe, blow, chill, dry — cognate with psyche, psychology, psychiatry; see ψυχή

ζῆλος (zêlos), eager rivalry, noble passion — cognate with jealous, zeal, zealot, zealous

κάτοπτρον (kátoptron), mirror — from κατά+ὀπτός+-τρον (an ending used to indicate an instrument)

μύωψ (múōps), shortsighted — cognate with myopia, myopic

σκηνή (skēnḗ), tent, stage — cognate with proscenium, scene, scenic

θεραπεύειν (therapeúein), to serve, obey, flatter, consult, heal — cognate with therapeutic, therapist, therapy; see θεράπων

λείπω (leípō), I leave — cognate with ec<u>lipse</u> and el<u>lipse</u>

ἄκανθα (ákantha), thorn, spine — cognate with acanthus (type of plants known for their spikes of flowers)

μεταλλικός (metallikós), metallic — cognates

List 12

δεινός (deinós), terrible, fearful — hence Dinornis, dinosaur

ὑγιής (hugiḗs), sound, healthy, hearty — hence hygiene, hygienic, hygienist

κενός (kenós), empty — hence cenotaph (empty tomb)

πρέσβυς (présbus), old man, elder, revered — hence presbyopia (deterioration of near vision with age), presbyter, Presbyterian, presbytery

γλαυκός (glaukós), gleaming, blue-green, gray — cognate with glaucoma, glaucous

ωχρός (ochrós), pale yellow, ochre, haggard — cognate with ochre, ochrous

πτερίς, πτερίδος (pterís, pterídos), fern — hence pteridology, pteridophyte, pteridosperm

κηρός (kērós), beeswax, honeycomb — cognate with kerosene

στίγμα (stígma), a mark, brand, tattoo — cognate with astigmatism, stigma, stigmatic, instigate, stick

κῆτος (kêtos), whale, sea-monster, abyss — hence cetacean, spermaceti

βοῦς (boûs), cow, ox, cattle — cognate with the bu- in bugloss (because the shape and roughness of its leaves resembles a cow's tongue), bulimia, buphthalmos, butter

σῆψις (sêpsis), putrefaction — cognate with antisepsis, sepsis

μάρσιππος (mársippos), bag, pouch — hence marsupial

κόπρος (kópros), dung, filth — hence coprolite, coprophagous, coprosma

σκέλος (skélos), leg — cognate with isosceles, triskelion

σηπτικός (sēptikós), septic — cognate with antiseptic, septic, septicaemia τύραννος (túrannos), absolute ruler — hence tyrannical, tyrannize, tyrannosaurus, tyranny, tyrant

ἄξιος (áxios), worthy, of like value — cognate with axiom, axiomatic

πυρετός (puretós), heat, fever — cognate with pyre, Pyrex, antipyretic

ζώνη (zṓnē), belt, sash — cognate with zone

πρίσμα (prísma), anything sawn, sawdust, prism — cognate with prism, prismatic

σύριγξ, σύριγγος (súrinx, súringos), pipe, tube, channel — cognate with syringa (because its stems were used for pipe-stems), syringe, syrinx

πόλος (pólos), pivot, hinge, axis, pole — cognate with pole (as in the north pole etc), polar, polhode, polos

στίζειν (stízein), to tattoo, mark — cognate with stigma, instigate, stick

σήπειν (sḗpein), to make rotten, to rot — cognate with sepsis, septic

Root Words

Directional

ἔνδον (éndon), in within
endo-, inside, within
e.g., endocardial, endocrine (+κρίνω), endogamy, endogenous, endoscopy, endoskeleton, endosperm, endospore

εἰς (eis), into
eis- / es- / is-, into
e.g., eisegesis (interpretation of word or passage in Scriptures by reading into it one's own ideas), episode (ἐπί+εἰς+ὁδός), isagoge (+ἄγω; introduction)

ἔσω (ésō), into, within
eso-, within
e.g., esophoria, esoteric (from ἐσωτερικός, belonging to an inner circle), esoneural (within the nerves), esoscopic (internal or interior concerns)

ἐκτός (ektós), without, outside
ecto-, outside
e.g., ectoblast (outer membrane of cell), ectoderm, ectogenesis, ectomorph, ectoplasm, ectotherm

ἔξω (éxō), out, out of, outside
exo-, outside
e.g., exoderm, exogamy (+γάμος), exoplanet, exoskeleton, exosome, exosphere, exoteric, exothermic, exotic, exotropia

πρό (pró), before, in front of
pro-, before, in front of
e.g., problem (from πρόβλημα, difficult question, set task; from προβάλλειν, to throw to, put forward), proboscis, prologue, prophet (+φημί), propolis (yes, the polis does refer to city, apparently because the material was used by bees to extend their hives), prostate, prow

πρός (prós), forward to, toward, by the side of
πρόσθεν (prósthen), before, in front of, earlier
pros- / proso-, forth, forward
e.g., proselyte, prosenchyma, prosobranch, prosody, prosopagnosia, prosophobia, prosopyle, prosthesis

διά (diá), through, between, after
dia-, apart, through
e.g., deacon (from διάκονος, messenger, courier), diagram, dialect, dialogue, dialysis, diameter, diapason (+πᾶς), diapause, diaphragm, diarrhoea, diaspora, diatonic, diatribe

παρά (pará), from, because of, beside, contrary to
par- / para-, beside, near
e.g., parable (from παραβολή, a placing side by side, comparison), parabola, parafovea, paradigm, paragon, parallel, parallelepiped (solid bounded by parallelograms), parameter, paranormal, paradox, parody

σύν (sún), beside, with
syn- / syl- / sym- / sys-, with
e.g., syllable, syllepsis, syllogism, symbiosis, symbol (+βάλλειν; from συμβάλλειν, to throw together), symmetry, sympathy, synagogue (+ἄγω; from συναγωγή, assembly; from συνάγειν, to bring together), synonym, synchronous, system (+ἱστάναι, to set up), systasis, systole (+στέλλειν; from συστέλλειν, to draw together, contract)

ἄκρος (ákros), extreme, outermost (especially of the top)
acro-, height, summit, tip
e.g., acrobat, acrocephaly, acrolect (the most prestigious dialect of a specific language), acromegaly, acromion, acronym, acrophobia, acropolis, acrostic

Comparative

ἕτερος (héteros), one or the other of two, either...or, different
heter-, different, other
e.g., heterochromatic (of several colours), heterodox, heterodoxy, heterodyne (+δύναμις), heterogeneity, heterogeneous, heteronym, heterophobia, heterosexual, heterosis, heterotic (to do with the manipulation of differences), heterozygous (+ζῦγόν)

ὁμός (homós), same, common, joint

hom-, same

e.g., homogeneous, homogenise, homograph (word spelt like another but of different meaning or origin), homologous, homology, homonym, homophobia, homophone, homophonic, homosexual, homozygous

ὅμοιος (hómoios), resembling, similar, shared, common, appropriate for, equal

homoe- / home-, like, similar

e.g., homeopathy / homoeopathy (contrast this with allopathy), homeostasis, homeothermy, homoiotherm, homoiothermic (warm-blooded, maintaining an almost constant body temperature)

ἴσος (ísos), equal to, same as, like

is- / iso-, equal, same

e.g., isobar, isochronous, iso-chromatic (of same colour), isocracy (system of government in which all have equal political power), isogloss, isograph, isomer, isometric, isomorphic, isosceles, isotonic, isotropic

μέρος (méros), part, component, share, member of a set

mer- / -merous, part

e.g., dimer, dimerous, heptamerous (having seven parts), heterodimer, hexamer, homodimer, isomer, isomeric, mereology (the study of the relations between parts and wholes), merismus, meromorphic, metamere, monomer, oligomer, polymer, telomere, tetramerous, trimer

πᾶς, all, every, each, whole; πᾶν (pân), *neuter form*

pan- / panto-, pa-, all

e.g., diapason (διά+), pan-American, panacea, pandemic, pandemonium, panoply (complete suit of armour), panoptic (seeing the whole at one view), panopticon, panorama, pantheism, pantograph, pantomime

τέλος (télos), completion, result, end

teleo- / tele-, complete

e.g., teleology, teleophobia (aversion to teleological explanations for natural phenomena), teleost (type of fish; +ὀστέον), telesis (intelligent direction of effort towards the achievement of a goal)

(not to be confused with the prefix tele- meaning *far*, although the Greek words are related)

Quality

ἀ- / ἀν-, a prefix used to give words the opposite meaning
an- / a- / am- / ar-
e.g., ambrosia, anaerobic, anhydrous, argon (+ἔργον), arrhythmia, atheism, atypical

δυσ- (dus-), bad, hard, unfortunate
dys-, badly, ill
e.g., dysentery, dysphagia, dysphasia, dysplasia, dystrophy

κᾰκός (kakós), bad, worthless, ugly, evil
κᾰκῐστος (kákistos), worst
caco- / cac- / kak-, bad
e.g., cachexy (+ἕξῐς), cacodemon / cacodaemon, cacodorous, cacodyl (organic compound with a disgusting smell), cacogenic, cacoglossia (putrid state of tongue), cacophony, cacosomnia, cacotrophy, kakistocracy

μῖσος (mîsos), hatred
mis-, hate
e.g., misandry, misanthrope, misogamy (+γάμος; hatred of marriage), misogynist, misogyny, misology (+λόγος; hatred of reason or knowledge), misoneism (+νέος; hatred of what is new)

εὖ (eû), well
eu-, good
e.g., eugenics, eulogy, euphemism, euphoria

καλός (kalós), beautiful, good
call- / cal-, beautiful
e.g., callicarpa (+κᾰρπός), calliope (literally beautiful-voiced), callisthenics, calligraphy, kaleidoscope

ὀρθός (orthós), straight, upright, safe, correct
orth-, straight
e.g., orthochromatic, orthodontia, orthodontist, orthodox, orthodoxy, orthoepy (+ἔπος; science of correct pronunciation of words), orthogonal, orthography (correct or conventional spelling), orthopaedics, orthoptic

στρεπτός (streptós), twisted
strepto-, twisted
e.g., Streptocarpus, streptococcus, streptomycete, streptomycin

ψευδής (pseudḗs), lying, false

pseudo-, false, deceptive

e.g., pseud, pseudo, pseudocoel, pseudocoelomate, pseudocyesis (false pregnancy), pseudocyst, pseudoephedrine, pseudomorph, pseudonym, pseudonymous, pseudoplastic, pseudopod, pseudoscience, pseudotumour

ἔτυμος (étumos), true, real

etym-, true

e.g., etymic, etymologic, etymologicon (an etymological dictionary), etymologist, etymologize, etymology

ὀξύς (oxús), sharp, pointed, quick, clever

oxy-, sharp, pointed

e.g., anoxia, dioxide, hypoxia, monoxide, oxide, oxygen, oxymoron (+μωρός), oxytocin, oxytone (word with acute accent on last syllable), paroxysm (παρά+)

ταχύς (takhús), swift, soon

tach-, swift

e.g., tachistoscope, tachyometer / tachymeter, tachycardia / tachyrhythmia, tachygraphy (art of quick writing), tachyon, tachyphylaxis

σοφός (sophós), clever, cunning, wise

soph-, wise

e.g., pansophism, pansophist, pansophy (universal knowledge), philosopher, philosophy, sophism, sophist, sophistry, sophisticated, Sophocles, sophomore, sophomoric

μωρός (mōrós), slow, dull, foolish, insipid

mor-, foolish, dull

e.g., moron, moronic, oxymoron (ὀξύς+), oxymoronic, sophomore, sophomoric, morosoph (wise fool or foolish pedant)

παχύς (pakhús), thick, stout, coarse, dull

pach-, thick

e.g., pachycephaly (abnormally thick skull), pachyderm (thick-skinned mammal), pachyodont (having thick or massive teeth), Pachysandra

βαθύς (bathús), high, deep, thick, strong

batho- / bathy-, deep, depth

e.g., batholith, bathometer, bathophobia, bathos, bathotic / bathetic, bathyal (pertaining to the zone between the continental shelf and the abyssal zone), bathymetric, bathyscaphe, bathysphere, isobathic

στερεός (stereós), firm, solid
stereo- / ster-, solid
e.g., allosteric, stereochrome, stereography, stereophonic, stereopsis, stereotaxis, stereotomy (science of cutting solids), stereotype (first meaning: method of printing using a solid plate of type-metal), stereotypical, steric (to do with the arrangement of atoms in a molecule)

σκληρός (sklērós), hard, harsh
scler-, hard
e.g., sclera, scleroid, scleroma, sclerenchyma, sclerite, scleritis, scleroderma, sclerometer, sclerophyllous, sclerosis, sclerotic, sclerous (related to skeleton, via a pre-Hellenic root meaning *to parch, wither*)

τραχύς (trakhús), jagged, prickly, rough
trach-, rough
e.g., trachea, tracheitis, tracheophyte, tracheostomy / tracheotomy, trachoma, trachyte (volcanic rock that's rough to the touch), Trachodon

εὐρύς (eurús), wide, spacious
eur-, wide
e.g., aneurysm (ἀνά+; from ἀνευρύνειν, to widen out), Europe, euryhaline, euryphagous (animals that eat a wide variety of foods or prey on a lot of different species), eurypterid, eurythermal, eurytopic (tolerant of a wide range of ecological habitats)

μέγας (mégas), big, great, mighty
mega- / megal-, great, large
e.g., acromegaly, megafauna, Megalithic, megacorporation, megacycle, megalomania, megalopolis, megaphone, megatherm, megaton (related to μεγάλος)

μικρός (mikrós), small
micr-, small
e.g., microaneurysm, microbe, microbial, microbiology, microcephaly, microcosm, microeconomics, micrography, micrometer, micron, microphage, microphone, microprocessor, microscope, microscopic

κλαστός (klastós), broken
κλᾰσῐς (klásis), action of breaking, fracture
clast- / -clase, broken
e.g., anaclasis, anorthoclase, antanaclasis, biblioclast, bioclast, clastic, euclase, iconoclast, oligoclase (ὀλίγος+), orthoclase, osteoclast, pyroclastic

καυστός (kaustós), burnt
caust- / caut-, burn
e.g., catacaustic (in maths, caustic describes a type of curve, so called because of the effect of light / heat intensity on different points), causalgia (+ἄλγος), caustic, cauterize, cautery,encaustic, holocaust, hypocaust

γλυκύς (glukús), sweet
glyc-, sweet
e.g., glycerine, glycerol, glycobiology, glycogen, glycogenesis, glycolysis (breakdown of sugars by enzymes), glycophyte, hypoglycaemia

ὑγρός (hugrós), wet, moist
hygro-, pertaining to liquids, moisture
e.g., hygrology, hygroma, hygrometer, hygrophilous, hygrophyte, hygroscope, hygrostat, hygrothermograph

γυμνός (gumnós), naked, unarmed, uncovered
gymn-, nude
e.g., gymnasium, gymnastics, gymnoplast, gymnosophist (+σοφός — one of an ancient Hindu philosophical sect who wore little or no clothing), gymnosperm, gymnospore

κρυπτός (kruptós), hidden, secret
crypt- / crypto-, hide, hidden
e.g., apocrypha, apocryphal, archaeocryptography, crypt, cryptanalysis, cryptic, cryptobiosis, cryptobiotic, cryptochrome, cryptogamy, cryptogenic, cryptography, cryptographic, cryptology, cryptomonad, cryptophyte, Cryptosporidium, cryptozoic, cryptozoology

ξένος (xénos), foreign, strange
xen-, foreign
e.g., axenic (denotes an organism without any life that is not itself), xenobiotic, xenoblast, xenogamy, xenogeneic (derived from an individual of a different species), xenograft, xenolith, xenology, xenon, xenophobia

καινός (kainós), new, novel, recent, fresh, strange
-cene / caino- / kaino-, recent, new
e.g., Anthropocene, Cainozoic / Cenozoic, encaenia , Eocene, Holocene, kainite, kainogenesis / kenogenesis, Miocene, Pliocene

παλαιός (palaiós), old, aged, ancient
palaeo- / paleo-, ancient, old
e.g., palaeobiology, palaeography (study of ancient writing), Palaeocene,

Palaeogene, Palaeolithic, palaeology, palaeomagnetism, palaeontology, Paleozoic

γέρων (gérōn), old man, old
ger-, old
e.g., erigeron (ἦρι, early+), geriatric (+ῑᾱτρός), gerontocracy (government by old men), gerontogeous (plants of the Old World), gerontology, gerontophilia, gerontophobia, gerusia (assembly of elders), progeria (related to γεραιός, γεραρός)

Number

δίς (dis), twice, doubly
di-, two
e.g., dicentric, dicephalous, dichotic (the dicho- prefix comes from δίχα meaning in two, apart), dichotomy, dichromic, dicotyledon, dicrotic (+κρότος, rattling noise; pulse showing a double beat for each heartbeat), digamy (second marriage), diode, dipole

διπλόος (diplóos), double
dipl-, twofold
e.g., diplodocus (+δοκός, a wooden beam), diploid, diploma (from δίπλωμα, a folded paper, letter of recommendation), diplomacy, diplomat, diplomatic, diplonema, diplophase, diplopia, diplotene, haplodiploidy

δεύτερος (deúteros), second of two, next
deuter- / deute-, deuto-, second
e.g., deuteragonist (character next in importance to the protagonist), deuteranopia, deuteride, deuterium, deuterogamist, deuterogamy (marriage a second time), Deuteromycota, deuteron, Deuteronomy, deuteropathy (secondary infection), deutencephalic, deutoplasm

ἀμφίς (amphís), on both sides, between
amphi-, both, on both sides of, both kinds
e.g., amphibian, amphibiology, amphibious, amphibole, amphigamous (without distinct sexual organs), amphioxus (+ὀξύς), Amphipoda, amphistyly, amphitheatre, amphora (because of having two handles)

ἥμισυς (hḗmisus), half
hemi-, half
e.g., hemianopia, hemichordate, hemicycle, hemihedron, hemimetabola (insects who undergo incomplete metamorphisis), hemimorphic,

hemiplegia, Hemiptera, hemisphere, hemispherectomy, hemistich

τέσσαρες (téssares) / τέτταρες (téttares), four
tetr- / tessa-, four
e.g., diatessaron, tetragon, tetrahedron, tetralogy, tetrameter, tetraphobia, tetrapod, tetrode

ὀλίγος (olígos), few, little, slight
olig-, few
e.g., oligarch, oligarchy, Oligocene, oligomer (polymer with up to 5 monomer units), oligodendrocyte, oligodendroglia (+δένδρον+γλία; a type of brain cell), oligopoly, oligosaccharide, oligotrophic / oligotropic

πολύς (polús), many, a lot of, great
poly-, many
e.g., polyandry, polyanthus, polychromatic, polygamy, polygamous, polyglot, polygon, polyhedron, polymath, polymer, Polynesia, polynomial, polyphonic, polyploid, polysaccharide, polytheistic
(note: οἱ πολλοί, the many)

μυρίος (muríos), numberless, infinite, endless
myri-, countless, ten thousand
e.g., myriad, myriagon (polygon with ten thousand sides), myriametre, myriapod

Colour

λευκός (leukós), bright, shining, white
leuc- / leuk-, white
e.g., aleukemia, aleukocytosis, leucism, leucocyte, leucopenia / leukopenia, leucoplast, leukemia, leukocytopenia, leucophore

μέλας (mélas), black, dark, evil
melan-, black, dark
e.g., melancholic, melancholy, Melanesia, melanin, melanization, melanoblast, melanocyte, melanogenesis, melanoma, melanophore, melanosis, melanosome, melatonin, neuromelanin

κυάνεος (kuáneos), dark blue
cyan- / cyano, blue
e.g., cyan, cyanic, cyanide, cyanobacterium, Cyanophyta, cyanosis, cyanotic, cyanotype (photographic process using cyanide)

χρῡσός (khrūsós), gold, something precious, gold coin
chrys- / chryso-, gold
e.g., chrysalis (from χρῡσαλλίς, a reference to the gold colour of many of these), chrysanthemum (+ἄνθος), chryselephantine (of gold and ivory), chrysoberyl, chrysolite, chrysoprase, helichrysum

Biology

γένος (génos), offspring, descendant, family, clan, gender
gen-, birth, beget, race, kind
e.g., allergen, antigen, autogenous, dysgenic, endogenous, epigenetics, erogenous, eugenics, exogenous, gene, genealogy, genesis, genetic, genocide, genotype, heterogeneous, homogeneous, hydrogen, pathogen (related to γένεσις, γενέτωρ, γένυς)

γόνος (gónos), that which is begotten, child, offspring, seed, fruit
gon- / -gony, pertaining to generation or development
e.g., archegonium, epigone, gonad, gonapophysis, gonorrhoea, oogonium, bibliogony, cosmogony, schizogony, theogony

ᾠόν (ōión), egg, seed
oo-, egg
e.g., epoophoron (ἐπί+ᾠόν+φορά), oidium, ooblast, oocyte, oogamous, oogamy, oogenesis, oogonium, ooid, oolite (type of limestone with small granules resembling fish roe), oolith, oology, oomycete, oophagy, oophorectomy, oophoritis (inflammation of an ovary), paroophoron

Plant

δένδρον (déndron), tree
dendr-, tree
e.g., dendrite, Dendrobium (+βίος), dendrochronology, dendrogram, dendrograph, dendroid, dendrology, dendromancy, Epidendrum, Philodendron, rhododendron, Toxicodendron

ξύλον (xúlon), cut wood, piece of wood, tree
xylo- / xyl-, wood
e.g., Dictyoxylon, haematoxylin, protoxylem, pyroxylin, xylan, xylem, xylene, xylocaine, xylograph (wood-engraving), xylol, Xylocarpus (+κᾰρπός), xyloid, xylophagous, xylophone, xylose

ὕλη (húlē), wood, trees, timber, substance, stuff, matter
-yl, used in chemistry to indicate a radical or functional group formed from a given molecule
e.g., acetyl, amyl, butyl, carbonyl, ethyl, hydroxyl, propyl

ἄνθος (ánthos), flower, bloom, scum
ἄνθεμον (ánthemon), flower, blossom
anth- / antho- / -anthem-, flower
e.g., anthemion (ornamental design using floral motifs), anther, anthocyanin (+κυάνεος), anthology (originally a gathering of flowers), Anthozoa, chrysanthemum (χρῡσός+), dianthus, hydranth (ὕδωρ+), perianth (structure forming the outer part of a flower), Zoantharia (ζωός+)

ῥόδον (rhódon), rose
rhod-, rose
e.g., cynorrhodon (dog-rose), rhodium, rhodochrosite (+χρῶμα), rhododendron, rhodonite, Rhodophyceae (red algae), rhodopsin, rhodora, rhodoxanthin, urrhodin (red pigment found in urine in certain conditions)

κᾰρπός (karpós), fruit, produce
-carp, fruit
e.g., acarpous, apocarpous, Callicarpa (καλός+), carpel, dipterocarp (δίς+πτερόν+), endocarp, gymnocarpous (γυμνός +), hemicarp, monocarp, mericarp (μέρος+), parthenocarpy, Podocarpus, polycarpous, Pterocarpus, sporocarp, Streptocarpus (στρεπτός+), syncarpous

μύκης (múkēs), mushroom or other fungus
myceto- / myco- / -mycete / -mycin, fungus
e.g., actinomycin, mycelium, mycetes, mycetoma, mycetophagous, Mycetozoa, mycobacterial, mycoflora, mycology, mycoparasite, Mycoplasma, mycorrhiza (+ρίζα), mycosis, mycotoxin, streptomycete (στρεπτός+), streptomycin, zygomycete (ζῡγόν+), zygomycosis

σάκχαρον (sákkharon), sugar
acchar-, sugar
e.g., disaccharide, lipopolysaccharide, monosaccharide, oligosaccharide, polysaccharide, saccharic, saccharide, saccharification, saccharin, saccharine, saccharolytic, saccharomycetes, saccharose, trisaccharide

σῖτος (sîtos), grain, corn, bread, food
sit-, food, grain, wheat
e.g., autosite, endoparasite, hyperparasitism, kleptoparasitism,

mycoparasite, parasite, parasitic, sitology, sitophobia, sitosterol, syssitia

οἶνος (oînos), wine

oeno-, relating to or resembling wine

e.g., oenochoe (type of jug used for wine in ancient Greece), oenocyte, oenologist, oenology / enology, oenomancy, oenomania, oenophile

(note that wine is also cognate)

βλαστάνειν (blastánein), to bud, sprout

blast- / blasto- / -blast, germ, embryo, bud, cell with nucleus

e.g., blastema, blastochyle, blastocœle, blastocyst, blastoderm, blastogenesis, blastoma, blastula, ectoblast, endoblast, entoblast, fibroblast, osteoblast, trophoblast (τροφή+)

φύω (phúō), I bring forth, produce, grow
φύσις (phúsis), origin, birth, nature, quality, type, property

(also related to φυή, φῦλον, φύλλον, φυτόν, φῦσῐκός)

physi- / -physis / physio-, nature

e.g., apophysis, epiphysis, Monophysite, physiocracy, physiognomy, physiology, physiotherapist, physiotherapy, physis, symphysis

σπείρω (speírō), to sow
σπόρος (spóros), a sowing, seed, harvest, offspring
σπορά (sporá), seed

speir- / spor-, sow

e.g., aplanospore, auxospore (αὐξάνω+), carpospore (κᾰρπός+), diaspora, endospore, exospore, homosporous, isosporous, leptosporangium, megasporophyll, microspore, microsporidian, microsporidiosis, sporadic, sporangiospore, sporangium, spore, sporocarp, Sporozoa

σπέρμα (spérma), seed, semen

sperm-, seed

e.g., angiosperm, aspermia, azoospermia, endosperm, gymnosperm, oligospermia, panspermia, Pteridospermatophyta (πτερίς+πτερίς+φυτόν), sperm, spermaceti, spermacide, spermatogenesis, spermatozoon, stenospermocarpy (production of seedless fruit)

ζευγνύναι (zeugnúnai), to yoke, join together
ζῠγόν (zugón), yoke
ζυγωτός (zugotós), yoked

zygo- / zyg-, denotes things that are paired or linked

e.g., dizygotic, heterozygote, heterozygous, homozygous, monozygotic, zeugma, zygaena (hammerheaded sharks), zygodactyl, zygoma, zygomatic, zygomorphic, Zygomycetes, zygon, zygosis, zygote

γάμος (gámos), marriage, wedding, matrimony
γαμέτης (gamétēs), husband
gam- / gameto-, marriage, reproduction
e.g., agamic, allogamy, apogamy (ἀπό+; asexual reproduction),
cleistogamic, cryptogam, deuterogamy, digamous, endogamous, exogamy,
gamete, gametogenesis, monogamous, polygamy

κοινός (koinós), common, public
κοίνωσις (koinosis), sharing
cœno- / -coenosis / -cenosis
e.g., coenobite (+βίος), cœnoblast, cœnocyte (+κύτος), cœnœcium
(+οἶκος), cœnosarc (+σάρξ), cœnosteum (+ὀστέον), phytocoenosis
(community of plants), koine (common language, a lingua franca)

κύτος (kútos), a hollow, a vessel
cyt- / -cyte / cyto-, cell
e.g., astrocyte, cytaster, cytokine (+κινεῖν), cytology, cytoplasm,
cytotoxin, leucocyte, leucocytosis, monocytopoiesis, pancytopenia,
polycythaemia (πολύς+κύτος+αἷμα), syncytium

ἀγγεῖον (angeîon), vessel, receptacle, body cavity
angio- / -angium, vessel
e.g., angioblast, angiocardiography, angiocarpous, angioedema,
angiogenesis, angiogram, angiography, angiology, angioma (tumour
produced by dilatation or formation of blood vessels), angioplasty,
angioscope, angiosperm, gonangium, lymphangitis, mesangium

μυελός (muelós), marrow, inmost part
myel- / myelo- / myelino-, relating to the spinal cord, relating to bone
marrow, relating to certain white blood cells
e.g., amyelia, myelin, myelinated, myelinopathy, myelinotoxic, myelitis,
myelographic, myeloid, myeloma, myelomeningocele, myelopathy,
myelopoiesis, myelosuppressive, poliomyelitis

γλία (glía), glue
glia-, glue
e.g., glia, gliadin, glial, glioblastoma, glioma, gliosis, gliotoxin, microglia

κόλλᾰ (kólla), glue
coll- / -col, having the nature or appearance of glue
e.g., collaemia (increased viscosity of blood; +αἷμα), collagen, collidine

(+εἶδος), colloid, collotype, eschatocol, protocol (from early meaning of the first sheet of a papyrus roll, bearing marks authenticating the papyrus)

Animal

κύων (kúōn), dog, bitch
cyno-, pertaining to dogs
e.g., cynic, cynical, cynocephalus (one of a fabled race of men with dogs' heads, also the Dog-faced Baboon), cynodont, dicynodont, Cynoglossum (plant genus; Hound's-tongue), Cynoidea, cynosure (+οὐρά; dog's tail = Ursa Minor, hence figurative meaning of something that provides guidance or direction, something that attracts attention), Procyon

ὄρνις (órnis), bird, chicken
ornith-, bird
e.g., Dinornis (δεινός+), notornis, Ornithischia (a division of dinosaurs), ornithoid, ornithology, ornithomancy, ornithopod, ornithopter, ornithorhynchus, ornithoscopy, ornithosis, ornithuric, steatornis

σαύρα (saúra), lizard
saur-, lizard, reptile
e.g., ankylosaurus, Apatosaurus, Brachiosaurus, Brontosaurus, dinosaur, hadrosaur, Pachycephalosaurus, plesiosaur, saurian, Saurischia, sauropod, saury (name applied to certain fish), tyrannosaurus

ὄφις (óphis), serpent, snake
ophi-, snake
e.g., ophicleide (a wind instrument), ophidian, Ophidion (eel-like fish), ophiolatry (+λᾰτρείᾱ), ophiolite (group of igneous rocks that includes serpentinite), ophiophagous (feeding on snakes), ophite, Ophiuchus (+ἔχω; constellation of a man holding a snake), Ophiura (+οὐρά)

σάρξ (sárx), flesh, body
sarc-, flesh
e.g., cœnosarc (κοινός+), perisarc, sarcasm, sarcastic, sarcocarp, sarcocele, sarcoid, sarcoidosis, sarcoma, sarcophagus, Sarcopterygii (class of fish characterized by fleshy fins), sarcosine, sarcosome

σῶμα (sôma), body, that which is material
soma- / -some, body
e.g., allosome, centrosome, chromosome, lysosome, macrosomia, mesosoma, metasomatic, microsomia, polysomic, prosoma, schistosome,

somaesthetic, somal, somatic, somatology, somatotopic, somatotroph, somatotype, somite, tetrasomic, trophosome, Trypanosoma, trisomy

στόμα (stóma), mouth, face, source of a river
stom- / -stome, mouth
e.g., actinostome, anastomosis, deuterostome, epistome, Gnathostomulida, hypostome, monostome (having only one mouth), peristoma, polystome, prostomium, protostome, stoma, stomach, stomatal, stomatic, stomatitis, stomatoplasty, stomatopod

τρῆμα (trêma), hole, aperture
trema-, hole
e.g., monotreme, pentremite (echinoderm with five spiracles around the mouth), peritreme (small ring around a breathing hole in some insects), trematode (presumably so called because their skin is often perforated by pores; from τρηματώδης having holes, perforated)

μίτος (mítos), thread of the warp, thread of destiny, string of a lyre
mit-, thread
e.g., dimity, mitochondrial, mitochondrion (+χόνδρος), mitogenesis, mitogenic, mitomycin (+μύκης), mitosis, mitosome, mitotic, samite (ἕξ+; 'six-threaded')

νῆμα (nêma), thread, yarn, silk
nema- / nemato- / -neme / -nema, thread
e.g., axoneme, leptonema (λεπτός+), myoneme (μῦς+), nema, nemata, nemaline, nematic, nematocyst, nematode (type of worm), nematology, pachynema (παχύς+), protonema, synaptonemal, treponema

χόνδρος (khóndros), lump, grain, cartilage
chondro-, pertaining to cartilage
e.g., achondroplasia, chondral, chondrify, chondrite, chondritis, chondrodite, chondroma, chondrostean (+ὀστέον), mitochondria (μίτος+)

μῦς (mûs), mouse, muscle
myo- / mys-, muscle
e.g., amyotrophy (atrophy of muscles), electromyogram, endomysium (one of the layers of tissue surrounding muscles), myocardium, myoglobinuria (presence of myoglobin in urine), myograph, myoid, myology, myoneme (+νῆμα), myopathy, myoplasm, myositis, perimysium
mu- / myo-, mouse
e.g., murine, musophobia / murophobia (fear of mice and rats), Myomorpha

οὐρᾱ́ (ourā́), tail

-oura- / -ura- / uro-, tail, posterior part

(uro- can also pertain to οὖρον, urine)

e.g., Anomoura (ἄνομος+), anthurium (ἄνθος+), anuran, colure, hypural, Menura (μήνη+), Ophiura (ὄφις+), sciurine, squirrel (from σκίουρος, which folk myth attributes to σκῑᾱ́+οὐρᾱ́, i.e., 'shadow-tail'), uraeus, uroboros / ouroboros, Urochordata, urogastric, uropodal, urosacral

ὄνυξ (ónux), claw, nail, hoof

onych- / -onyx, pertaining to nails or claws

e.g., Deinonychus, koilonychia (condition known as spoon-nail), Megalonyx (genus to which ground sloth belongs), mesonychid, onychogryphosis (excessive thickening and curvature of nails), onychopathy, onychophagia (habit of biting one's nails), onyx, sardonyx

ἕρπειν (hérpein), to move slowly, creep

herp-, creep

e.g., herpes (the original Greek word for shingles, ἕρπης, meant a creeping), herpetic, herpetiform, herpetoid (like a reptile), herpetology, herpetotomy (dissection of reptiles), herpolhode (+πόλος+ὁδός; found in geometry)

(note that this word is also cognate with serpent)

Mineral

πέτρα (pétra), cliff, cave, stone

petr-, rock

e.g., glossopetra, osteopetrosis, petrifaction, petrify, petrochemical (relating to the chemistry of rocks), petrogenesis, petroglyph, petrographic, petrography, petroleum (mineral oil), petrology, petrous

λίθος (líthos), stone

litho- / lith- / -lite, stone (the use of -lite for mineral terms comes from French, who over time substituted this for the older term -lithe)

e.g., aerolith (old word for a meteorite), chromolithography, chrysolite (χρῡσός+), endolith, epilithic (growing on stone), ijolite, lithic, lithography, lithology, lithophone, lithophyte, lithosphere, lithotomy, megalith, Mesolithic, microlite, monolith, monolithic, Neolithic, Paleolithic, phonolite (because it made a ringing sound when struck)

ἤλεκτρον (ḗlektron), amber, alloy of gold and silver
electr- / electro-, amber, pertaining to electrons or electricity
e.g., catelectrotonus (κατά+ἤλεκτρον+τόνος), electric, electrical, electricity, electride, electrification, electrify, electrocardiogram, electrocatalysis, electrocute, electrocyte, electrode, electrogenesis, electrogenic, electrogram, electrolysis, electrolyte, electromagnetic, electron, electronic, electrophile, electrophoresis, electroshock, electrum, polyelectrolyte

ἄνθραξ (ánthrax), charcoal, carbuncle
anthrac- / anthra- / anthraco-, coal
e.g., anthracene, anthracite, anthracnose, anthraconite, anthracosaur, anthracosis, anthracycline, anthrax

ἅλς (háls), salt, brine, sea, wit
ἅλινος (hálinos), saline
hal- / halo-, salt
e.g., halcyon (originating in a Greek myth that this mythical bird nested on the sea), halide, halieutic (pertaining to fishing), haliotis (a genus of shells, so called because of their resemblance to a human ear), halite, halogen, haloid, halomancy, halometer, halophile, halothane, isohaline, mixohaline (μιξο-+; brackish), thermohaline

Human

ἄνθρωπος (ánthrōpos), human being, humanity
anthrop-, human
e.g., Anthropocene (+καινός), anthropocentric, anthropogenic (relating to human origins), anthropology, anthropometry, anthropomorphic, anthroposophy, misanthrope, philanthropy

πίθηκος (píthēkos), ape
pithec-, ape, monkey
e.g., Aegyptopithecus, Ardipithecus, australopithecine, Australopithecus, cercopithecus, Dryopithecus, Gigantopithecus, Pithecanthropus (+ἄνθρωπος), pitheciine, pithecoid, Pliopithecus, Ramapithecus

παῖς, παιδός (paîs, paidós), child, son, daughter, young person
paed- / ped- / paedo- / pedo-, child
e.g., orthopaedics, paediatric, paedodontic, paedogenesis, paedological,

paedomorphosis, paedophilia, pedagogue, pedagogy

παιδείᾱ (paideíā), upbringing, teaching, education
-paedia, education, learning
e.g., cyclopaedia, encyclopaedia, hypnopaedia, paideia

παρθένος (parthénos), maidenly, chaste
parthen-, virgin
e.g., parthenic, parthenium, parthenocarpy (+κᾰρπός), parthenogenesis, parthenogenic, Parthenon (dedicated to Athena, also known as Athena the Virgin), parthenospore, parthenote

ὄντος (óntos), actual, real, being
onto-, relating to being or existence
e.g., ontogenesis, ontogenetic, ontogenic, ontogeny, ontography (study of the human response to the natural environment), ontological, ontologist, ontology, ontotheological

ἴδιος (ídios), private, pertaining to self, peculiar, specific
idi- / idio-, own, individual, peculiarity
e.g., idioblast, idiochromatic, idiogram, idiolect, idiom, idiomorphic, idiopathic, idiopathy, idiophone, idiosome, idiosyncrasy (+σύν+κρᾶσῐς), idiosyncratic, idiothetic (+θετῐκός), idiot, idiotic

Mind

μνήμη (mnḗmē), memory, remembrance
mne-, memory
e.g., amnesia, amnesiac, amnesty, anamnesis (recalling of things past), anamnestic, Mneme, mneme, mnemonic, mnemotechnic

βίβλος (bíblos), papyrus, book
bibl- / biblio-, book
e.g., bible, biblioclasm, biblioclast (+κλαστός; destroyer of books), bibliogony (+γόνος; production of books), bibliographic, bibliography, biblioklept, bibliolatry, bibliology, bibliomancy, bibliomania, bibliophile, bibliophobe, bibliophobia, bibliotaph (one who buries books by keeping them locked up; +τᾰ́φος)

σῆμα (sêma), mark, sign, token
sema-, sign
e.g., aposematic, polyseme, polysemic, polysemous, polysemy, semantic,

semantics, semaphore, semasiology, sematic, seme, sememe, semiotic, semological, semotactic, tetraseme, triseme, trisemic

ποιεῖν (poieîn), to make, create, produce, compose, consider
ποιητής (poiētḗs), maker, inventor, composer
(also ποίημα)
poie- / poe-, make
e.g., melopoeia, onomatopoeia, poem, poesy, poet, poetaster (inferior poet), poetic

πράττειν (práttein), to do, practice
πρᾶξις (prâxis), deed, action, work, conduct, practice
πρᾶγμα (prâgma), a thing done, fact
prag- / prac- / -praxia, do, practice
e.g., apraxia, dyspraxia, echopraxia, parapraxis, practic, practical, practice, practician, pragma, pragmatic, pragmatism, pragmatist, praxeology, praxis

γλύφειν (glúphein), to carve, engrave, note down
glyph- / glypho-, carve
e.g., aglyphous, anaglyph, glyph, glyphic, glyphography, glyptic, Glyptodon, glyptography, hieroglyph, hieroglyphic, monotriglyph, petroglyph, proteroglyphous, triglyph

φίλος (phílos), that which is loved or important, friend
φιλία (philía), friendship, love
phil- / -phile, love of, friendship, loving
e.g., basophil, bibliophile, drosophila (a type of fruit fly, 'dew-loving'), gypsophila, halophile (ἅλς+), haemophilia, hydrophilic, hygrophilous (ὑγρός+), necrophilia, paedophilia, paraphilia, Philadelphia, Philadelphus, philanderer, philanthropy, philately, philia, philharmonic, Philodendron, philology, philosophy, philter / philtre

λᾰτρείᾱ (latreíā), service, worship
-olatry / -latry / -later / -latrist / -latrous, worship of
e.g., astrolatry, anthropolatry, autolatry, bibliolater, bibliolatry, cosmolatry (worship of the world), demonolatry, dendrolatry (δένδρον+), epeolatry, gastrolater, geolatry, gynolatry, iconolatry, ideolatry, idolater, idolatrous, idolatry, litholatry, logolatry, monolatry (worship of one god, esp. when others assumed to exist), monolatrous, necrolatry, pyrolatry, symbololatry, theolatry

τᾰ́φος (táphos), funeral rite, burial, tomb
-taph, tomb, burial
e.g., bibliotaph, cenotaph (κενός+), epitaph (ἐπί+; from ἐπιτάφιον, funeral oration; from ἐπιτάφιος, over the grave), taphonomy (study of the processes by which remains become fossilized), tritaph (group of three chambers in a prehistoric tomb)

θάνατος (thánatos), death, corpse
thanas- / thanato-, death
e.g., athanasy (immortality), euthanasia, thanatocoenosis, thanatoid, thanatology, thanatophilia, thanatophobia, thanatophoric, thanatopsis, Thanatos

κλέπτειν (kléptein), to steal, cheat, mislead, conceal
κλέπτης (kléptēs), thief
klept-, steal
e.g., biblioklept, kleptobiosis, kleptocracy, kleptomania, kleptomaniac, kleptoparasitism

πωλεῖν (pōleîn), to sell, levy taxes, betray
-poli / -poly / -pole, sell, pertaining to merchants
e.g., bibliopole, duopoly, monopolist, monopolize, monopoly, oligopoly

Body

ἐγκέφᾰλος (enképhalos), inside the head, brain
(from κεφαλή) (note that εν becomes εγ before γ, κ, χ)
encephal-, pertaining to the brain
e.g., encephalitis, encephalitogenic, encephalogram, encephalopathy, mesencephalic, metencephalon, neencephalon, paleencephalon, prosencephalon, rhombencephalon, telencephalon

ῥίς, ῥινός (rhís, rhinós), nose, snout
rhin- / -rhine, nose, snout
e.g., catarrhine, mesorrhine, otorhinolaryngology, platyrrhine, rhinoceros, rhinology, rhinophyma, rhinoplasty (+πλαστός), rhinoscopy, rhinosinusitis, rhinosporidiosis, rhinovirus

βρόγχος (brónkhos), trachea, windpipe, throat
bronch- / broncho-, windpipe
e.g., bronchia, bronchial, bronchiectasis (dilatation of the bronchial

tubes), bronchiole, bronchiolitis, bronchitis, bronchophony, bronchopneumonia, bronchoscope, bronchotomy, bronchus

γαστήρ (gastḗr), belly, womb, stomach, appetite

gastro- / gastr-, stomach

e.g., epigastric, epigastrium (ἐπί+; part of the abdomen immediately above the stomach), epigrastriocele, gastric, gastrin, gastritis, gastroenterologist, gastrolith, gastronome, gastronomy, gastropod, gastroptosis, gastroscope, gastrula

χείρ (kheír), hand

chir- / cheir-, of the hand or hands

e.g., allochiria, cheiranthus (+ἄνθος), chiral, chirality, chirapsy (touching or rubbing with hand), chiroid, chiropodist, chiropractic, chiroptera, chirurgy, enchiridion (handbook), epicheirema, Haplocheirus

δάκτυλος (dáktulos), finger, toe

dactyl-, digit, finger, toe

e.g., arachnodactyly, brachydactyly, dactyl, dactylic, dactylology, dactylomancy, dactylomegaly, dactylus, dactyly, didactyly, ectrodactyly, heterodactyly, leptodactylous, monodactyly, oligodactyly, pentadactyly, perissodactyl, polydactyly, pterodactyl, schizodactyly, syndactylous, tetradactylous, tridactyly, zygodactyly

μᾰστός (mastós), human breast

masto- / -mastia, breast

e.g., mastalgia (+ἄλγος), mastectomy, mastodynia (+ὀδύνη), mastopathy, mastopexy, gynaecomasty, micromastia, pleiomastia, polymastia

ὗστέρᾱ (hustérā), uterus, womb

hystero- / hyster-, womb, associated with hysteria

e.g., hysteralgia, hysterectomy, hysteria, hysterical, hysteritis, hysteroid, hysteropexy, hysterophyte, hysterotomy (=Caesarean section)

μήτρᾱ (mḗtrā), womb

(from μήτηρ, mother)

metro-, pertaining to the uterus; -metrium, denoting different layers of tissue in the uterus

e.g., endometrium, mesometrium, metritis, metropathia, metrophlebitis, metrorrhagia (+ῥηγνύναι), myometrium, parametrium

(note there are multiple uses of metro- as a prefix, the main one relating to measurement, and the second one relating to city transportation)

ὄρχις (órkhis), testicle, ovary, orchid
orchi-, testicle, orchid
e.g., cryptorchid, mesorchium, orchid, orchidopexy / orchiopexy, orchidology, orchidomania, orchidophile, orchiectomy, orchitis

κύστις (kústis), bladder
cyst- / cysti- / cysto-, cyst, bladder
e.g., cystalgia (+ἄλγος), cysteine, cystic, cysticercus, cystine, cystinosis, cystitis, cystocarp (+κᾰρπός), cystolith, cystoma, oocyst, polycystic

θάλαμος (thálamos), inner chamber, bedroom, bed
thalam-, chamber, bed
e.g., epithalamion, hypothalamus, prothalamion, thalamencephalon, thalamic, thalamifloral, thalamocortical, thalamotomy, thalamus

φλέψ (phléps), vein
phlebo-, pertaining to veins
e.g., phlebitis, phlebogram, phlebography, phlebolith, phlebology, phlebosclerosis, phlebotomist, phlebotomize, phlebotomy, thrombophlebitis

Senses

αἴσθησῐς (aísthēsis), sensory perception
αἰσθητικός (aisthētikós), sensitive, perceptive, (of things) perceptible
aesth- / -aesthesia / esthesia, feeling, sensation
e.g., aesthesic (relating to sensory perception), aesthesis, aesthete, aesthetics, anaesthetic, anaesthesia, dysaesthesia (difficulty of sensation), synaesthesia

σκέπτεσθαι (sképtesthai), to look at, examine
σκοποῦ (skopós), watcher, guardian, spy, target
scept- / scop-, look at, examine, view, observe
e.g., diascope (διά+; magic lantern), endoscopy, kaleidoscope, macroscopic, microscope, periscope, sceptic / skeptic, sceptical, scope, scopophilia (voyeurism), stereoscopic, stethoscope, telescope, telescopic, Telescopium (constellation)

δρᾶν (drân), to act, take action
δραστικός (drastikós), efficient, active
δρᾶμα (drâma), a deed, act, a play
dram- / dras-, do
e.g., drama, dramatic, dramaticle (miniature or insignificant drama),

dramatist, dramatize, dramaturge, dramaturgy, drastic, drastically, melodrama, melodramatic, monodrama

μίμος (mímos), mime, actor, imitation

(from μιμέομαι)

mim- / mimeo-, repeat, copy

e.g., mime, mimeograph, mimesis, mimetic, mimeticism, mimic, mimicker, mimicry, mimographer, neuromimetic, pantomime, psychotomimetic

φαίνειν (phaínein), to cause to appear, to show

phan- / phanero- / phen- / -phane, to show, visible

e.g., cellophane, diaphanous, diphenyl, epiphany, euphenics, fantasy / phantasy, fenestra, defenestrate, glaucophane (γλαυκός+), hierophant (ἱερός+), homophene, phanerogam, phanerophyte, phanerozoic, phanopoeia (use of words in poetry to suggest visual images), phantasm, phantasmagoria, phantasmal, phantom, phene, phenetic, phenology, phenomenon, phenotype, phosphene (φῶς+), sycophant, theophany, tryptophan

φᾰσῐς (phásis), appearance

-phasis, appearance, visibility

e.g., diphasic, emphasis, phase, phasis, prophase, telophase

(but note same word with different meaning)

εἰκών (eikṓn), figure, likeness, image

icon- / icono-, image, icon

e.g., aniseikonia, eikonal, icon, iconic, iconoclasm, iconoclast, iconography, iconolater, iconology, iconomachy, iconostasis

εἶδος (eîdos), form, image, shape, appearance, type

id- / eid- / -oid, shape, form, picture

e.g., blastoid, cardioid, choroid, collidine (κόλλᾰ+), diploid, eidetic, eidolon, eidos, glenoid, helicoid, idol, idolater, idolatry, idyll, idyllic, kaleidoscope, nuclide, pareidolia, trochoid, xiphoid

(related to idea)

ὀσμή (osmḗ), smell, scent, stench

osm-, odor

e.g., anosmia, anosmic, coprosma (κόπρος+), Diosma (δῖος+), dysosmia, dysosmic, euosmia, hyperosmia, hyperosmic, hyposmia, hyposmic, Osmanthus, osmic, osmium, osmoceptor, osmology, osmophore, parosmia

οὖς (oûs), ear, hearing; pl. ὦτα

ot-, ear

e.g., microtine, Myosotis (Mouse-ear), otalgia, otic, otitis, otocyst, otolaryngologic, otolith, otology, otologist, otopathy, otoplasty, otorhinolaryngology, otorrhea, otosclerosis, otoscope, otoscopy, parotic (παρά+; situated beside the ear), parotid, periotic

ἠχέω (ēkhéō), to sound, ring
ἠχώ (ēkhṓ), echo, reflected or protracted sound

ech- / echo-, sound

e.g., anechoic, catechesis (from κατηχεῖν, to instruct orally; from κατά+ἠχέω), catechism, catechist, catechize, catechumen, echo, echocardiography, echoencephalography, echogram, echoic, echolalia (+λᾰλῐᾱ́), echolocation, echometer, echopraxia (+πρᾶξις)

φάναι (phánai), to speak, say
φημί (phēmí), I speak, say, agree
φήμη (phḗmē), prophetic voice, rumour, reputation

e.g., defamed, fame, famous, phatic, pheme, phememe, prophet

φωνή (phōnḗ), sound, a cry, speech, language

phon- / -phone, sound

e.g., allophone, antiphon, cacophony, diaphony, euphony, homophone, ideophone, idiophone (percussion instrument made of material that is itself capable of making a sound when struck), megaphone, microphone, monophonic, morphophonology, phonaesthesia (+αἴσθησῐς; sound symbolism), phone, phoneme, phonetic, phonics, phonogram, phonograph, phonology, polyphonic, stereophonic, symphony, telephone

φᾰσῐς (phásis), utterance, speech

-phasia, denoting disorders of speech

e.g., aphasia, heterophasia, paraphasia
(but note same word with different meaning)

φθέγγεσθαι (phthéngesthai), to make a sound, utter, shout, singng
φθόγγος (phthóngos), a sound or voice

phtheg- / -phthong, utter

e.g., apophthegm / apothegm (pithy or sententious maxim), apophthegmatic, diphthong, monophthong

ἔπος (épos), something spoken: speech, story, song

ep- / epo-, usually something to do with epics, esp. epic poetry

e.g., epeolatry (+λᾰτρείᾱ; worship of words), epic, epoist, epopee, epopoeia, epos, epyllion (miniature epic), orthoepy (ὀρθός+)

μῦθος (mûthos), something said, speech, conversation, advice, story, legend

myth-, pertaining to story or legend

e.g., myth, mythic, mythical, mythification, mythoclastic (that which discredits a myth), mythogeny, mythography, mythologem, mythologize, mythology, mythomania, mythopoeia, mythos, stichomythia (στίχος+)

λέγειν (légein), to say, speak, mean

leg- / -lect, say, language

e.g., dialect, dialectic, dialectologist, dialectology, prolegomenon

λέξῐς (léxis), word, explanation, way of speaking

λεξῐκός (lexikós), pertaining to words

λεξικόν (lexikón), lexicon

-lexia / -lexic / lexico-, pertaining to words

e.g., alexia, alexithymia,dyslexia, dyslexic, lexeme, lexical, lexicography, lexicology, lexicon, lexigram, lexigraphy, lexis, paralexia, relexification (also connected to λόγος)

Digestion

ὀρέγειν (orégein), to reach, stretch, give, desire

oreg-, reach

e.g., anorectic, anorexia, anorexic, dysorexia, orectic (relating to appetite), orexigenic, orexin, parorexia

πέψις (pépsis), digestion

πεπτός (peptós), digested

pept- / -pepsis, digest

e.g., dyspepsia, dyspeptic, eupepsia / eupepsy, eupeptic, monopeptide, oligopeptide, pepon, pepsin, peptic, peptide, peptone, polypeptide, tetrapeptide, tripeptide

φαγεῖν (phageîn), to eat

phago- / -phagy / -phagous, eat, feeds on or in such a way

e.g., autophagosome, autophagy, bacteriophage, coprophagous (κόπρος+), dysphagia, geophagy (practice of eating earth), hyperphagia, macrophage, oesophagus / esophagus, phagocyte, phage, polyphagia, sarcophagus

Medical

ῐ̄ᾱτρός (īātrós), physician, surgeon
iatro- / -iatric /-iatry, pertaining to medicine
e.g., iatrochemist, iatrogenic, iatromathematical (relating to a mathematical theory of medicine), iatromechanics, iatrophysics, bariatric, paediatric, geriatric, physiatry, podiatrist, podiatry, psychiatrist, psychiatry

ἄλγος (álgos), pain, that which causes pain
-algia / -algy / alge- / algo-, pertaining to pain
e.g., algedonic (+ἡδονή), algesia, algometer, algophobia, antalgic, cardialgy, causalgia (καυστός+), glossalgia, hysteralgia, ischialgia, myalgia, neuralgia, nostalgia (νόστος, returning home+)

ὀδύνη (odúnē), pain, distress
odyn-, pain
e.g., allodynia, anodyne, hysterodynia (ῠ̔στέρᾱ+), mastodynia, odynophagia, pleurodyne

πάθος (páthos), pain, suffering, misfortune, emotion, condition
path-, feeling, disease
e.g., antipathy, apathetic, apathy, empathy, empathize, encephalopathy, homeopathy, idiopathic, pathetic, pathogen, pathogenesis, pathogenic, pathologist, pathology, pathos, psychopath, sympathetic, sympathy

αἷμα (haîma), blood
haema- / hema- / haemato- / -haemia, blood
e.g., anaemia, haemangioblastoma (+ἀγγεῖον+βλαστάνειν), haematopoiesis (+ποίησις), haematology, haematoma, haematuria (blood in the urine), haemoglobin, haemophilia, haemophobia, haemorrhage, haemorrhoid

ἔμεσις (émesis), vomiting
ἔμετος (émetos), vomiting, vomit
emes- / emet-, vomiting
e.g., antiemetic, emesis, emetia, emetic, emetine, emeto-cathartic, haematemesis, hyperemesis

σπεῖρα (speîra), anything twisted or wound, wreath, coil, twist
spiro-, twisted, spiral
e.g., spiral, Spirochaete, spirochaetosis, spirograph, spirogyra, spiroid, spironolactone, spiroplasma

ὄγκος (ónkos), bulk, volume, tumor, molestation, dignity
onco-, relating to swelling or tumours
e.g., oncofetal, oncogenesis, oncogenic, oncolite (a spheroidal type of rock), oncologist, oncology, oncolytic, oncotic

κρίνω (krínō), to separate, divide, judge
-crine, relating to glandular secretion
e.g., apocrine (ἀπό+), eccrine (from ἐκκρίνειν, to secrete; from ἐκ+κρίνω), eccrinology, eccritic (promotes secretion), endocrine, endocrinology, exocrine, holocrine, merocrine
(from κρίσις)

γλῶσσα (glôssa) / γλῶττα (glôtta), tongue, language
gloss- / glot- / -glossia, tongue, language
e.g., aglossal, diglossia, epiglottis, gloss, glossary, glossography, glossolalia, glossology, glossophobia, glossoplegia, glossotomy, glottis, heteroglossia, idioglossia, isogloss, monoglot, monoglottism, polyglot

Politics & Power

ἄρχω (árkhō), to begin, to rule
arch- / arche- / archi-, ruler
e.g., anarchist, anarchy, archangel, archetype, architect, archon, autarch (αὐτός+; absolute ruler), eparchy (ἐπί+), exarch, gynarchy (γυνή+; government by a woman or women), monarch, navarch (ναῦς+; commander of a fleet), oligarchy, patriarchy, plutarchy

δύναμις (dúnamis), power, strength, ability, authority
dyna- / dynamo- / -dyne, power
e.g., aerodynamic, autodyne, didynamous, dyname, dynameter, dynamic, dynamically, dynamism, dynamite, dynamize, dynamo, dynamogeny, dynamograph, dynamometer, dynamotor, dynast, dynastic, dynasty, dyne, geodynamics, heterodyne

κράτος (krátos), might, strength, power
-cracy / -crat, government, rule, authority
e.g., akrasia (lack of physical strength, weakness of will), akratic, aristocracy, autocracy, autocrat, autocratic, bureaucracy, democracy, democratic, gynaecocracy, pancratium, plutocracy, technocracy, technocrat, theocracy

σθένος (sthénos), strength, might, power
sthen-, strength
e.g., asthenia, asthenic (weak, debilitated), asthenosphere, callisthenic / calisthenic, callisthenics, hypersthene, hyposthenia, sthenia, sthenic

στρατός (stratós), army, military force
strat-, army
e.g., strata, stratarchy, stratagem, strategy, stratocracy, stratography, stratonic, stratum, stratus
(related to στρατηγία)

στρῶμα (strôma), mattress, bed
stroma- / -strome, spread, strew
e.g., biostrome, blastostroma, olistostrome, stroma, Stromateus (genus of flat fish), stromatolite, Stromatoporidae, xylostroma
(the connection is through the pre-Hellenic root meaning of *to spread, to extend* — as shown through *stratum*)

τόξον (tóxon), bow (weapon), rainbow, arc
tox- / toxo- / -toxin, bow-shaped, poisonous (the link is through poison for smearing on arrows)
e.g., aflatoxin, antitoxin, autotoxin, intoxicate, neurotoxin, tox, toxic, toxicology, toxin, Toxodon, toxology, toxophilite, toxoplasmosis

κρίσις (krísis), decision, judgment, trial, dispute
crit- / crisi-, judge, separate
e.g., crisis, criterion, critic, critical, criticaster (petty critic), criticize, criticism, critique, diacritic, hypercriticism, hypocrisy, hypocrite, kritarchy, Kritosaurus, syncrisis

νέμω (némō), to deal out, dispense, distribute, pasture the flocks
e.g., archnemesis, nemesis, Nemesis (goddess of retribution, i.e., dispenser of justice)

νομός (nomós), pasture, food, distribution, dwelling
e.g., nomad, nomadic, Numidia

νόμος (nómos), custom, law
-nomy, arrangement, law
e.g., agronomy, antinomy, astronomy, autonomous, autonomy, bionomics, economics, economy, gastronomy, metronome, nome, nomology, nomothetic, numismatics (from νόμισμᾰ, coin; from νομίζω, to use customarily), polynomial, taxonomy

ἄνομος (ánomos), lawless
anomo-, something with irregular aspect
e.g., anomobranchiate, anomocarpous, anomodont, anomophyllous, anomorhomboid, anomouran, anomy / anomie

κόσμος (kósmos), order, government, fashion, universe, world
government, fashion, universe, world
cosm-, universe
e.g., acosmism (doctrine that the universe doesn't exist, or is not distinct from God), cosmic, cosmogenic, cosmogony, cosmographer, cosmologist, cosmology, cosmonaut, cosmoplastic (moulding or forming the universe), cosmopolis, cosmopolitan, cosmopolite, cosmos, cosmosphere, cosmothetic (assumes an external world; +θετἴκός), cosmotron, microcosm, macrocosm
κοσμεῖν (kosmeîn), to order, arrange, adorn
cosmet-, art of dress and ornament
e.g., cosmetic, cosmetician, cosmetics, cosmetologist, cosmetology

τάσσειν (tássein), to arrange, put in order, undertake, command
τάξις (táxis), arrangement, ordering, battle array, brigade
τάγμᾰ (tágma), command, order, arrangement
tag- / taxo- / -taxis / -tactic, arrange, order
e.g., ataxy, chemotaxis, epitaxy, homotaxial, phonotactic, phonotactics, phototaxis, rheotaxis (ῥεῖν+), syntactic, syntagma, syntagmatic, syntax (from συντάσσειν, to put together in order), tactic, tagma, tagmeme, taxidermy, taxis, taxonomy, thermotaxis

ἔχω (ékhō), I have, possess, hold, withhold
ἕξἴς (héxis), state of having, state of being
ech- / -exy, denoting holding or (confusingly) withholding
e.g., cachexy (κᾰκός+), echard (water in the soil which is not available to plant roots), entelechy (ἐν+τέλος+; complete expression of some function; that which gives perfection to something), ephectic (ἐπί+; characterized by suspense of judgment), epoch (ἐπί+), eunuch, synechia, synocha

στίχος (stíkhos), row of soldiers, line of poetry
stich-, line, row
e.g., acrostic, distichous (arranged in two opposite rows), hemistich, monostich, stich, sticheron, stichic, stichomancy (divination by lines of verse from books taken at random), stichomythia, telestich, tristich

Gods

ἅγιος (hágios), devoted to the gods, sacred, holy

hagio- / hagi-, holy, saintly

e.g., hagiocracy, hagiographical, hagiography, hagiolatry (worship of saints), hagiology, hagioscope

ἱερός (hierós), supernatural, holy, sacred

hier-, holy, sacred

e.g., hierarch, hierarchy, hieratic (of the priests), hierocracy, hieroglyph, hieroglyphic, hierogram / hierograph (sacred inscription), hierolatry, hierophant (+φαίνειν; initiating priest), hierurgy (a sacred performance)

δῖος (dîos), heavenly, divine

dio-, pertaining to Zeus or something heavenly

e.g., Dianthus (+ἄνθος), dioscuric, Diosma (+ὀσμή), eudiometer, Zeus (also cognate with divine, deity)

Places

πόλις (pólis), city, community
πολιτικός (politikós), civic, public, social

poli- / -polis, city

e.g., acropolis, cosmopolitan, geopolitics, megalopolis, metropolis, necropolis, police, policy, politic, politician, politics, polity, propolis (apparently because it's used by bees to maintain the structure of their hives), Tripoli

τόπος (tópos), place, location, topic, position

topo- / -tope / -topia, place, location

e.g., atopic, biotope, dystopia, ectopic, isotope, homotopic, polytope, topic, topocentric, topography, topology, toponomastic (pertaining to place names), toponym, toponymy, topos, toposcope, utopia

γῆ (gê), land, earth, country

ge- / geo-, earth

e.g., apogee, geocentric, geode, geodesic, geography, geoid, geology, geomancy, geometry, geomorphology, geophysicist, geophyte, geopolitics, georgic (ἔργον+; rustic, relating to agriculture), geostatic, geostationery, geostrophic (+στρέφειν), geosynchronous, geosyncline, hypogeous (underground), hypogeum, Pangea, perigee

νῆσος (nêsos), island
-nesia / -nese, island
e.g., Austronesian, Chersonese (a peninsula, esp. the Thracian peninsula), Indonesia, Micronesia, nesidioblast, Peloponnese, Polynesia

πέλαγος (pélagos), sea
pelag-, sea
e.g., abyssopelagic, archipelago, bathypelagic, mesopelagic, pelagian, pelagic, pelagite

σπήλαιον (spélaion), cave
σπῆλυγξ (spêlynx), cave
spele- / spelyng-, cavern, cave
e.g., spelaean, speleologist, speleology, speleothem, speluncar, spelunk, spelunker

Physics

χρόνος (khrónos), time, period, term, lifetime
chron- / chrono-, time
e.g., anachronism, asynchronous, biochronology, chronaxie (+ἄξιος), chronic, chronicle, chronobiology, chronology, chronometer, chronoscope, heterochrony, isochron, synchronize, synchronous, tautochrone (ταὐτο+)

Light

οὐρανός (ouranós), vaulted sky, home of the gods, universe
uran-, heaven, sky
e.g., uranic (heavenly, vs earthly), uraninite, uranium, uranography, uranology, uranometry, uranophane, Uranus

ἡμέρᾱ (hēmérā), day
hemera-, day
e.g., ephemera, ephemeral, ephemeron, ephemerous, hemera, hemeralopia (day-blindness)

σελήνη (selénē), moon, month
selen-, moon
e.g., paraselene, Selene, selenite, selenium, selenography, selenology

φῶς, φωτός (phōtós), light

photo- / phos- / -phote, pertaining to light

e.g., holophote, phosgene, phosphene (+φαίνειν), photic, Photinia (from φωτεινός shining, bright), photino, photo, photoallergy, photoautotroph, photocopy, photogenic, photograph, photolyase, photon, photopsia, photosensitive, photostat, photosynthesis, phototactic, telephoto

φωσφόρος, bringing or giving light, morning star

phosphoro-, relating to phosphorus

e.g., phosphor, phosphoresce, phosphorescent, phosphorolysis, phosphorous, phosphorus, phosphoryl, phosphorylase, phosphorylate

ἀκτῖς (aktîs), ray, beam

actin- / actino-, pertaining to light or to radial symmetry or rays

e.g., actin, actinic, actinium, actinobacillosis, actinograph, actinolite, actinometer, actinomorphic, actinomycete, actinopterygian, Actinozoa

χρῶμα (khrôma), skin, colour, complexion

chro- / chrom-, color

e.g., achromatopsia, amphichroic, apochromat (ἀπό+;improved form of an achromatic lens), auxochrome (αὐξάνω+), chromaesthesia (a form of sound-colour synaesthesia), chromatic, chromatid, chromatograph, chromatophore, chrome, chromium, chromolithography, chromophore, dichroic, hyperchromasia, monochrome, polychromy, trichromatic

φλέγειν (phlégein), to set on fire, burn, inflame
φλέγμᾰ (phlégma), flame, fire, heat, inflammation
φλόξ (phlóx), flame

phlegm- / phlog-, burn, heat, inflammation

e.g., phlegm, phlegmatic, phlegmonous, phlogistic (inflammatory; of the nature of phlogiston), phlogiston (hypothetical substance once supposed to exist in all combustible bodies), phlogogenic, Phlox, phloxine

θερμός (thermós), hot, boiling, hotheaded

therm-, heat, warm

e.g., thermal, ectotherm, endotherm, exothermic, geothermic, hyperthermia, hypothermia, isotherm, therm, thermal, thermite, thermocline, thermocouple, thermode, thermodynamic, thermohaline, thermometer, thermophil, thermos, thermostat, thermotropic

(related to θέρμη)

Shape

μορφή (morphḗ), shape, form, appearance, outline, kind
morph-, form, shape
e.g., amorphous, anthropomorphism, dysmorphic, dysmorphophobia, ectomorph, endomorph, geomorphology, homeomorphic, isomorphic, mesomorph, metamorphic, metamorphosis, morpheme, Morpheus, morphine, morphology, morphosyntactic, pseudomorph, theriomorphic

γῦρος (gûros), ring, circle
gyr- / gyro-, ring, round
e.g., autogiro, giro, gyre, gyrectomy, gyrocopter, gyroidal, gyrolite, gyromagnetic, gyromancy, gyrophoric, gyroscope, gyrose, gyrostat, gyrostatic, gyrus, magnetogyric, microgyria, spirogyra (+σπεῖρα)

κύκλος (kúklos), circle, ring, sphere, marketplace, crowd
cycl- / cyclo-, circle
e.g., anticyclone, bicycle, cycle, cyclical, cyclone, cyclops, eccyclema, encyclopaedia (ἐν+κύκλος +παιδείᾱ+), epicycle, hemicyclium, hypocycloid, polycyclic, pseudocyclosis, tetracyclic, tricycle, unicycle

σφαῖρα (sphaîra), ball, globe, sphere
spher- / -sphere, ball
e.g., aspheric, atmosphere, barysphere, hemisphere, hypersphere, mesosphere, planisphere, pseudosphere, sphaeroblast, sphere, spherical, spherocyte, spheroid, spherometer, spherulite, stratosphere

ῥόμβος (rhómbos), bullroarer, anything which may be turned or spun, spinning motion, rhombus
rhomb-, in the shape of a rhombus
e.g., rhomb, rhombencephalon (division of the brain), rhombic, rhombicuboctahedron, rhombifer (Cuban crocodile), rhombohedral, rhomboid, rhomboideus (a muscle in the back), rhombus, rhumb

λεπίς, λεπίδος (lepís, lepídos), scale, flake, shell
lep- / lepido-, flake, peel, scale
e.g., lepal, lepidine, lepidoid, lepidolite, Lepidoptera (+πτερόν), lepidopterist, lepidote, lepidotrichia, lepra, leprosy, osteolepiform

λεπτός (leptós), fine-grained, thin, lean, narrow, slight, small, delicate
lepto-, small, delicate
e.g., antilepton, leptin, leptocephalus, leptokurtic, leptome, leptomonad,

lepton, leptophyllous, leptosomic, leptospira, leptotene

στῦλος (stûlos), pillar, column
stylo-, column
e.g., astylar, axostyle (ἄξων+), diastyle, epistyle, eustyle, hexastyle, orthostyle, peristyle, prostyle, style, stylite, stylo (referring to members of plant genus Stylosanthes), stylobate, stylohyoid, styloid, stylolite, stylus

πόρος (póros), passage-way, opening, ford, strait, journey, filament
por- / poro- / -pore, passage
e.g., aporetic (inclined to doubt; from ἀπορεῖν, to be at a loss, from ἄπορος, impassable), aporia, aporose (not porous), blastopore, emporium, pore, porencephaly (condition characterized by one or more cyst-like spaces in the brain), poriomania (impulsive, aimless wandering), porismatic, porocyte, porokeratosis (+κέρας), porosis, porosity, porous

ὁδός (hodós), threshold, path, way, journey, method
hod- / od- / -ode, path, way
e.g., anode (ἀνά+), cathode (κατά+), diode, electrode, episode, ergodic, exodus, heptode, herpolhode (ἕρπειν+πόλος+), hexode, hodograph, hodometer / odometer, hodoscope, hydathode, method, methodical, Methodist, methodology, period, periodic, synod, tetrode, triod, zincode
ὁδαῖος (hodaîos), on or by the road
e.g., proctodeum, rhynchodaeum, stomodaeum, urodaeum

Action

κινεῖν (kineîn), to set in motion, meddle, change, cause
κίνησις (kínēsis), motion, dance, revolution
κίνημα (kínēma), movement
kine- / cine-, movement, motion
e.g., akinesia, cineradiography, cineaste (lover of cinema, filmmaker), cinema, cinematic, cinephile, Cinerama, cytokine, dyskinesia (δυσ+), hyperkinetic, hypokinesis, kinaesthesia (+αἴσθησῖς), kinase, kinescope, kinesiologist, kinesis, kinetic, kinin, lymphokine, photokinesis, telekinesis

χορεία (khoreía), dance, chorea
chore-, relating to dance
e.g., choir, choral, chorale, chorea, choreal, choree, choreography, choreology, chorus, hemichorea

χορός (khorós), dance ring, chorus, choir
chor-, pertaining to a band of singers
e.g., choir, choral, chorale, chorus

πλανᾶν (planan), to lead astray, to wander
πλανήτης (planḗtēs), wanderer
plan- / plano-, errant, free-living
e.g., aplanatic (free from aberration), aplanogamete, aplanospore, exoplanet, planet, planetary, planetarium, planetismal / planetesimal, planetoid, planetology, planoblast, planogamete, planospore, protoplanet

ἄγω (ágō), I lead, fetch, carry off
ago- / agogue, carries off, guide
e.g., agogic (relates to musical tempo), agometer, agon, cholagogue (χολή+; medicine that carries off bile), demagogue, hydragogue, pedagogue, mystagogue, synagogue, glucagon, hypnagogic

ἡγέομαι (hēgéomai), I go before, lead the way, command, rule
heg- / -egesis, lead
e.g., diegesis (διά+; a narrative), diegetic, eisegesis (εἰς+), exegesis, exegete, exegetic, hegemon, hegemonic, hegemony, hegumen

βαίνω (baínō), to walk, go, step
-βάτης (-bátēs), one who walks on whatever described in the first part of the word
-bat, to do with walking on or moving
e.g., acrobat, adiabatic, diabetes, hyperbaton ('over-stepped'; a figure of speech in which the usual word order is inverted), stereobate, stylobate (also connected to base, basis)

τρέχειν (trékhein), to run, to run over
τροχός (trochós), wheel, hoop, ring, island, perimeter, race
trech- / troch-, run, wheel
e.g., ditrochee, epitrochoid, hypotrochoid, trochaic, trochanter, trochee, trochelminth, trochilus, trochlea, trochlear, trochoid, trochus

δρόμος (drómos), race, running, racetrack, course
-drome, course, track
e.g., aerodrome, catadromous (going down the river to spawn), dromedary (the breed is bred for racing), dromond, dromos (passage to a temple or other building), dromotropic, homodromous, palindrome (πάλιν+), prodromus, syndrome ("runs with"; set of concurrent symptoms)

ἵστημι (histēmi), to make to stand, to stand
sta- / ste-, cause to stand
e.g., statine, episteme, epistemic, epistemology, orthostatic, prostate, stasimon, stater, statoblast, statocracy, statolatry, system (from σύστημα, whole composed of several parts, literary composition, organized body, series of musical intervals), systematic, systemic, thermostat

στᾰτῐκός (statikós) causing to stand
e.g., antistatic, apostasy, apostate, cholestasis (χολή+), diastatic, ecstasy, ecstatic, epistasis, electrostatic, homoeostasis, hydrostatic, hypostasis, hypostasize, hypostatic, hypostatize, isostatic, metastasis, metastasize, orthostatic, stasis, static, systasis
(also related to στατός, στάσις)

στήλη (stélē), upright stone, post, engraved stone
-stele, engraved stone, botany: the central cylinder within vascular plants
e.g., actinostele (ἀκτῑς+), eustele, protostele, stela, stele

στρέφειν (stréphein), to twist
στροφή (strophḗ) , a turning
streph- / stroph- / strob- / stromb-, turn
e.g., anastrophe, antistrophe, apostrophe, boustrophedon, catastrophe, catastrophic, diastrophism, epistrophe, exstrophy, geostrophic, monostrophe, monostrophic, strophe, strophic

τρέπειν (trépein), to turn
τρόπος (trópos), a turn, manner, trope, mode
trep- / trop- / tropo- / trope, turn
e.g., allotrope, ectropion / ectropium, entropy, heliotrope, isentropic, isotropic, phototropic, pleiotropic, polytropic, protrepsis, psychotropic, thermotropic, treponeme, treponematosis, troparion, trope, tropic, tropism, tropology, tropomyosin, tropopause, troposphere, zoetrope

φέρειν (phérein), to bring, bear, carry
pher- / phor- / -phore, bear, carry
e.g., anaphora, cataphoric, dysphoria, epiphora, esophoria, euphoria, metaphor, periphery, pheromone, phosphor, prophoric, prosphora, pyrophoric, tocopherol
(also related to φορά)

φόρησις (phórēsis), being carried, the act of bearing
-phoresis, movement of small particles by some force
e.g., cataphoresis, diaphoresis (from διαφόρησις, perspiration, from διαφορεῖν, to carry off), electrophoresis, phoresis, phoresy, photophoresis

στέλλω (stéllō), to make ready, prepare, dispatch, summon, fetch
stell- / stol-, send
e.g., apostle (from ἀπόστολος, messenger), diastole, diastolic, epistle (from ἐπιστέλλειν, to send a message), epistolary, epistolography, peristalsis, peristaltic, stole (noun), systaltic, systole, systolic

λαμβάνειν (lambánein), to take, grasp, seize, catch, keep
-labe, denotes instruments that take measurements, or names of visual pigments in the retina; -lab-, in syllable and its offshoots
e.g., astrolabe, chlorolabe, cosmolabe, cyanolabe, erythrolabe, mesolabe, nocturlabe, octosyllabic, syllabic, syllabism, syllable (σύν+), syllabogram, trisyllabic, trisyllable

λῆψις (lêpsis), seizure
-lepsy / -leptic, seizure; -lepsis, usually refers to something rhetorical
e.g., analepsis (remaining meaning is that of a flashback in a story), analeptic, catalepsy, cataleptic, epilepsy, epileptic, metalepsis, narcolepsy, nympholepsy, prolepsis, proleptic, proslepsis, syllepsis, theolepsy

λῆμμα (lêmma), premise, assumption
-lemma, assumption, argument
e.g., analemma, analemmatic, dilemma, dilemmatic, lemma, lemmatize

τιθέναι (tithénai), to put, place, deposit, pay
the-, put
e.g., hypothec, logothete, thesaurus (from θησαυρός, treasure, vault)

θετός (thetós), placed, put, settled, adopted

θετῐκός (thetikós), fit for placing, apposite, to do with a thesis
-thesis / -thetic / -thetical, positing
e.g., antithesis, bibliothetic (relating to the arrangement of books on a shelf), epenthesis, epithet, hypothesis, idiothetic (ἴδιος+), monothetic, nomothetic (νόμος+), parenthesis, parenthetic, prosthesis, prosthetic, prothetic (posited before, prefixed), synthesis (from σύνθεσις, composition, logical synthesis), synthetic, thesis, antithetical, hypothetical (also related to θέσις, θέμα)

πίπτειν (píptein), to fall, throw oneself down

πτῶσις (ptôsis), falling, a fall, grammatical case
pto-, fall
e.g., anaptotic, asymptomatic, apoptosis, diptote (a noun with only two cases), peripeteia, peripety, proptosis, proptotic, ptomaine (from πτῶμα, fallen body, corpse), ptosis (drooping of the upper eyelid), symptom (from σύμπτωσις, exposed to chance, from σύν+πτῶσις), symptomatic

ῥεῖν (rheîn), to flow, stream

rheo- / rhoea, flow, pertaining to excessive flow or secretion
e.g., amenorrhoea, diarrhoea, endorheism / endoreism, galactorrhoea, gonorrhoea, haemorrhea, logorrhoea, otorrhoea (ὦτα+), rheid, rheology, rheometer, rheophyte (plant that lives in flowing water), rheostat, rheotropic, rheum, rheumatic, rheumatism, rheumatology, rhyton
(also related to ῥυθμός)

ῥηγνύναι (rhēgnúnai), to break asunder, tear, rend

rhag- / rheg-, rend, tear
e.g., haemorrhage / hemorrhage, haemorrhagic, lymphorrhagia, menorrhagia (μήνη+), metrorrhagia (μήτρᾱ+), pneumorrhagia, psychorrhagy, regma, rhagades, rhegma, rhegmatogenous, rhexis

τέμνειν (témnein), to cut, hew, maim, butcher
τόμος (tómos), slice, piece, tome

tem- / tom-, cut
e.g., anatomy, apotemnophilia, atom, atomic, autotomy, diatom, dichotomy, entomology (from ἔντομᾰ, insects, because their bodies are divided into segments), entomophagous, epitome, lithotomy, monatomic, pentatomic, polytomy, temenos, tmesis, tome, tomography, trichotomous

ἐκτέμνειν (ektémnein), to cut out, cut down, castrate
ἐκτομή (ektomḗ), excision

-ectomy, operation to remove a part
e.g., appendicectomy / appendectomy, colectomy, embolectomy, hysterectomy, iridectomy, lobectomy, tonsillectomy, vasectomy

πλήσσειν (plḗssein), to strike, smite, am stricken
πλῆγμα (plêgma), blow, stroke

pleg-, strike
e.g., apoplectic, apoplexy, cataplectic, cataplexy, diplegia, hemiplegia, monoplegia, paraplegia, paraplegic, plangent, plectrum, pleximeter / plessimeter, tetraplegia

τύπτειν (túptein), to beat, strike

typo- / -type, stamp, model
e.g., allotype, archetype, ecotype, ectype, heterotypic, homotypic, isotype, lectotype, logotype, monotypic, neotype, paratype, phenotype, prototype, schizotypic, somatotype, stratotype, syntype, type, typography, typology
(related to τύπος)

πνεῖν (pneîn), to blow, breathe
pne-, blow, breathe, lung
e.g., anapnograph, anapnoic, apnœa / apnea, dyspnœa, metapneustic, pleuropneumonia (πλευρά+), pneumatic, pneumatocyst, pneumatology, pneumococcal, pneumocystosis, pneumonectomy, pneumonia
(related to πνεῦμα)

σφύζειν (sphúzein), to throb, beat
σφυγμός (sphugmós), throbbing of inflamed parts, beating of heart, earthquake
σφύξῐς (sphúxis), pulse
sphyg-, pulse
e.g., asphyxia, asphyxiate, sphygmograph, sphygmology, sphygmomanometer

τείνειν (teínein), to stretch, extend, spread
taeni- / -tene, ribbon
e.g., diplotene, hypotenuse, leptotene, neoteny, pachytene, taenia, taeniasis (infestation with tapeworms), taeniosome, taenite, zygotene
τετανός (tetanós), muscular spasm
τόνος (tónos), rope, cord, chord, note
ten- / ton-, stretch
e.g., atonic, baritone, catatonia, catatonic, decatonic, diatonic, dystonia, hexatonic, hypotonia, isotonic, microtone, monotone, monotonous, monotony, oxytone, pentatonic, peritoneum, polytonal, syntonic, tetanolysin, tetanospasmin, tetanus, tetany, tetratonic, tone, tonic, tonofibril, tonology, tonometer, tonotopic, tune
τᾰσῐς (tásis), stretching, tension
-tasis, tension
e.g., entasis (from ἐντείνειν, to strain), epitasis, protasis, tasimeter
ἐκτείνω (ekteínō), to stretch out, to prolong
ἔκτᾰσῐς (éktasis), extension
-ectasis, extension, dilatation
e.g., atelectasis (ἀ-+τέλος+; imperfect dilatation), bronchiectasis, cystectasy, ectasis, lithectasy, phlebectasis

σπᾶν (spân), to draw, tug
σπᾰστῐκός (spastikós), drawing in, absorbing
σπασμός (spasmós), spasm, convulsion
spasm- / spast-, convulsive, contraction
e.g., antispasmodic, palinspastic, perispomenon, spasm, spasmatic,

spasmodic, spasmogenic, spasmolytic, spasmoneme, spasmophilia (undue tendency of muscles to contract), spastic

τρέφειν (tréphein), to thicken, congeal, increase, make to grow
treph- / troph- / tropho-, feed, grow
e.g., atrophy, autotrophic, auxotrophy, dystrophy, heterotroph, hypertrophy, lipodystrophy, mammotrophin, photoheterotroph, phototrophic, prototrophy, saprotroph, trophectoderm, trophic, trophoblast, tropholytic, trophonema, trophotropic
(related to τροφή)

κρᾶσῐς (krâsis), mixture, union, temperature, temperament
-cras, mixture
e.g., acrasin, crasis, dyscrasia, hippocras (ὑπο+; mixed together lightly), idiosyncrasy, polycrase, theocrasy (mingling of deities or divine attributes into one personality; mixture of worship of different deities)

λύειν (lúein), to loose, loosen, release, dissolve
λύσις (lúsis), loosing, emptying, releasing
ly- / lyo- / lysi- / -lysis / lytic-, dissolving
e.g., analyse, analysis (ἀνά+; from ἀνάλυσις, act of loosing, fact of dissolving, resolution of a problem), analytic, autolysis, catalyse, catalyst, catalytic, dialysis, electrolysis, electrolyte, glycolytic, Hippolyte, hydrolytic, lyochrome, lyotropic, lysergic, lysigenous, lysine, lysis, lysol, lysosome, lytic, palsy, paralyse, paralysis, paralytic, proteolysis
(note that solve, dissolve, resolve, are also cognate with these words)

σείειν (seíein), to shake, agitate
σεισμός (seismós), shaking, earthquake, storm, agitation
sei-, shake; seismo-, relating to earthquakes
e.g., aseismic, helioseismology, meizoseismal (relating to the point of maximum disturbance; μείζων means greater, from μέγας), microseism, microseismic, seismic, seismogram, seismograph, seismology, seismometer, seismonasty, seismotectonic, sistrum, teleseismic

πλαστός (plastós), formed, moulded
-plasty, moulding or grafting of a body part
e.g., angioplasty, arthroplasty, osteoplasty, otoplasty, rhinoplasty, stomatoplasty, tympanoplasty

Complete Review List

Use this list for any later reviews once you've worked through the book. This complete list is in alphabetical order, so you can also use this, if you wish, to quickly check whether any specific word is included.

-βᾰτης

ἀ- / ἀν-

ἄβυσσος

ἀγγεῖον

ἅγιος

ἀγνωσῐᾱ

ἀγρός

ἄγω

ἀγωνία

ἀγωνιστής

ἄημι

ᾱήρ

ἄθεος

ἀθλητής

ᾱθλητῐκός

ᾱθλον

αἰεί

αἰθήρ

αἷμα

αἴσθησῐς

αἰσθητικός

αἰών

ἄκᾰνθᾰ

ἄκρος

ἀκτῑς

ἄλγος

Ἀλέξανδρος

ἄλινος

ἄλλος

ἅλς

ἁμαρτή

ἀμβροσία

ἀμνησία

ἀμνίον

ἄμφῑς

ἀνά

ἄνᾰβᾰσῐς

ἀνάλυσις

ἄνᾰφορᾱ

ἀνδρόγυνος

ἄνεμος

ἀνευρύνειν

ἀνήρ   ἀριθμός

ἄνθεμον   ἄριστος

ἄνθος   ἀρκτικός

ἄνθραξ   ἄρκτος

ἄνθρωπος   ἄρμα

ἀνομία   ἁρμόζω

ἄνομος   ἁρμονία

ἀνορεξία   ἁρμός

ἄντα   ἄρτι

ἀντί   ἀρχιτέκτων

ἀντίθεσις   ἄρχω

ἄξιος   ἀστήρ

ἄξων   ἀτμός

ἀπό   αὖ

ἀποθεόω   αὐθεντικός

ἀποθέωσις   αὐξάνω

ἀποθήκη   αὔρᾱ

ἀποκαλύπτω   αὐτάρ

ἀποκάλυψις   αὖτε

ἀπορεῖν   αὐτόματος

ἄπορος   αὐτός

ἀπόστολος   βαθύς

ἄρα   βαίνω

ἀράχνη   βακτηρία

ἀρετή   βάκτρον

ἀρθρῖτις   βαλλίζω

ἄρθρον   βάλλω

βᾰρεῖᾰ

βαρύς

βάσις

βῐβλῐοθήκη

βίβλος

βίος

βιοτή

βλαστάνειν

βόλος

βοτάνη

βουλῑμία

βοῦς

βρᾰχῑων

βρόγχος

βυθός

γάλακτος

γαλαξίας

γαμέτης

γάμος

γαστήρ

γένεσις

γενέτωρ

γένος

γένυς

γεραιός

γεραρός

γέρων

γῆ

γῆρας

γιγνώσκειν

γλαυκός

γλία

γλυκύς

γλύφειν

γλῶσσα

γλῶττα

γνάθος

γνώμων

γνῶσις

γνωτός

γόνος

γόνυ

Γραικός

γράμμα

γραμματικός

γρᾰμμή

γραπτός

γραφεύς

γραφή

γράφω

γυμνάζω

γυμνός

γυνή

γῦρος

δαίμων

δάκτυλος

δεινός

δέκα

δέμω

δένδρον

δεξιτερός

δέρμα

δεσπότης

δεύτερος

δημᾰγωγός

δημοκρᾱτῐ́ᾱ

δημοκρᾰτῐκός

δῆμος

διά

δῐᾰρροῐᾱ

διαφορεῖν

διαφόρησις

διδάσκω

δῖος

διπλόος

δίς

δίχα

δόγμα

δογματικός

δόμος

δόξᾱ

δόσις

δοτός

δούξ

δρᾶμα

δρᾶν

δραστικός

δρόμος

δύναμις

δύο

δυσ-

ἐγκέφᾰλος

ἐγώ

ἕδρᾱ

ἐθνικός

ἔθος

εἰ

εἶδος

εἰκών

εἶναι

εἰς

ἐκ

ἑκατόμβη

ἑκατόν

ἐκκρίνειν

ἔκστᾰσῐς

ἔκτᾰσῐς

ἐκτείνω

ἐκτέμνειν

ἐκτομή

ἐκτός

ἕλιξ

ἔμβρῠον

ἐμέ

ἔμεσις

ἔμετος

ἐν

ἔνδημος

ἔνδον

ἐνέργεια

ἐνεργός

ἔνθεος

ἐνθουσῐασμός

ἐνθουσῐαστής

ἐννέα

ἐντείνειν

ἔντερον

ἔντομᾰ

ἕξ

ἐξήγησις

ἕξῐς

ἔξω

ἐπιστέλλειν

ἐπιτάφιον

ἐπιτάφιος

ἔπος

ἐποχή

ἑπτά

ἐπώνυμος

ἔργον

ἕρπειν

ἔρως

ἔσω

ἐσωτερικός

ἑτερογενής

ἕτερος

ἔτυμος

εὖ

εὑρίσκειν

εὐρύς

εὐφρασία

ἔχω

ζευγνύναι

Ζεύς

ζῆλος

ζῠγόν

ζυγωτός

ζύμη

ζῳδῐᾰκός

ζώνη

ζῷον

ζωός

ἡγεμονίᾱ
ἡγεμών
ἡγέομαι
ἡδονή
ἠθικός
ἠθολογίᾱ
ἠθολόγος
ἤλεκτρον
ἥλιος
ἡμέρᾱ
ἡμι-
ἥμισυς
ἧπαρ
ἡπᾰτῐ́ζων
Ἡρακλῆς
ἡρωίνη
ἥρως
ἠχέω
ἠχώ
θάλαμος
θάνατος
θαῦμα
θέατρον
θέμα
θεοκρᾱτίᾱ
θεός
θεραπεύειν

θεράπων
θέρμη
θερμός
θέσις
θετῐκός
θετός
θεώρημα
θεωρίᾱ
θεωρός
θηλή
θήρ
θηρῐ́ον
θησαυρός
Θησεύς
θυγάτηρ
θύρα
θώρᾱξ
ῑᾱτρός
ἰδέᾱ
ἴδιος
ἰδιώτης
ἱερός
ἱππόδρομος
ἱπποπότᾰμος
ἵππος
ἴσος
ἵστημι

ἱστορία

ἱστορικός

ἵστωρ

καί

καινός

καίτοι

κᾰ́κῐστος

κακοι

κᾰκός

καλός

καλύπτω

Καλυψώ

κάρα

καρδιά

κᾰρπός

κατά

κᾰτᾰ́βᾰσῐς

καταγράφω

κατηχεῖν

κάτοπτρον

καυστός

κενός

κέντρον

κέρας

κεφαλή

κῆρ

κηρός

κῆτος

κινεῖν

κίνημα

κίνησις

κλαστός

κλέπτειν

κλέπτης

κλίμα

κλῑμᾰκτηρῐκός

κλῖμαξ

κλίνη

κλίνω

κοινός

κοίνωσις

κόλλᾰ

κόπρος

κοσμεῖν

κόσμος

κρανίον

κρᾶσῐς

κράτος

κρῐ́νω

κρίσις

κρυπτός

κυάνεος

κύκλος

κύλινδρος

κῠνῐκός

κύστις

κύτος

κῠ́ων

κῶνος

λάκκος

λᾰλῐᾱ́

λαμβάνειν

λᾰτρείᾱ

λέγειν

λείπω

λεξικόν

λεξῐκός

λέξῐς

λεπίς, λεπίδος

λεπτός

λευκός

λῆμμα

λῆψις

λίθος

λίνον

λίπος

λογῐσμός

λογῐστῐκός

λόγος

λύγξ

λύειν

λύσις

μάθημα

μᾰθημᾰτῐκός

μᾰκροθῡμῐᾱ

μᾰκρός

μάμμη

μανίᾱ

μᾰντείᾱ

μάρσιππος

μάσταξ

μᾰστῐχᾰ́ω

μᾰστός

μέ

μεγᾰ́λος

μέγας

Μέδουσᾱ

μείζων

μεῖον

μέλας

μέρος

μεσοποτάμιος

μέσος

μετά

μεταλλικός

μέταλλον

μεταφέρω

μέτρον

μήνη
μήτηρ
μήτρᾱ
μηχανή
μηχανικός
μικρός
μιμέομαι
μῖμος
μῖσος
μίτος
μνήμη
μόνος
μορφή
μυελός
μῦθος
μύκης
μύλη
μυρίος
μῦς
μύσταξ
μύστης
μύωψ
μωρός
νάρκη
ναῦς
ναυσία
ναύτης

ναυτία
ναυτικός
νεκρός
νέκταρ
νέκυς
Νέμεσις
νέμω
νέος
νεῦρον
νεφρός
νῆμα
νῆσος
νομός
νόμος
νόστος
ξένος
ξύλον
ὀβελίσκος
ὄγκος
ὀδαῖος
ὀδός
ὀδούς
ὀδύνη
ὄζειν
οἱ
οἱ πολλοί
οἰκέω

οἰκονομίᾱ

οἶκος

οἶνος

ὀκτώ

ὀκτώπους

ὀλίγος

ὅλος

ὄμμα

ὅμοιος

ὁμός

ὀμφαλός

ὄνομᾰ

ὀνομᾰτοποιΐᾱ

ὄντος

ὄνυξ

ὀξύς

ὀπτικός

ὅραμα

ὄργανον

ὀρέγειν

ὀρθός

ὄρνιθος

ὄρνις

ὄρυζα

ὀρφανός

ὄρχις

ὀσμή

ὀστέον

ὅτι

οὐρᾱ́

οὐρανός

οὖρον

οὖς

ὀφθαλμός

ὄφις

ὄψις

πάθος

παιδᾰγωγός

παιδείᾱ

παῖς, παιδός

παλαιός

πάλιν

Πάν

παρά

πᾰρᾰβᾰ́λλω

παραβολή

παράδεισος

πᾰρᾰ́δοξος

παρένθεσις

παρθένος

πᾶς

πατήρ

πατριώτης

παχύς

πέλαγος

πέντε

πέπερι

πεπτός

πέρᾱ

πέρᾱν

περί

Περικλῆς

πέταλον

πετάννῡμι

πέτασος

πέτομαι

πέτρα

πέψις

πιέζειν

πίθηκος

πῖνον

πίπτειν

πλανᾶν

πλανήτης

πλάσμᾰ

πλάσσω

πλάστης

πλαστῐκός

πλαστός

πλᾰτύς

πλευρά

πλῆγμα

πλήσσειν

πλοῖον

πλοῦτος

πνεῖν

πνεῦμα

ποιεῖν

ποίημα

ποίησις

ποιητής

πολεμεῖν

πολιός

πόλις

πολιτικός

πόλος

πολύς

πομπή

πόρνη

πόρος

πορφύρεος

ποταμός

ποτήρῐον

πούς

πρᾶγμα

πρᾶξις

πράττειν

πρέσβυς

πρεσβύτερος

πρίν

πρίσμα

πρό

προβάλλειν

πρόβλημᾰ

πρόγραμμα

Προμηθεύς

πρόμος

πρός

πρόσθεν

πρότερος

πρωΐ

πρῶτος

πτερίδος

πτερόν

πτερόω

πτέρυξ

πτερωτός

πτυχή

πτῶσις

πύλη

πῦρ

πυρετός

πωλεῖν

ῥάδιξ

ῥεῖν

ῥεῦμα

ῥηγνύναι

ῥίζα

ῥινόκερως

ῥίς, ῥινός

ῥόδον

ῥόμβος

ῥυθμός

σάκχαρον

σάρξ

σαύρα

σείειν

σεισμός

σελήνη

σῆμα

σήπειν

σηπτικός

σῆψις

σθένος

σῖτος

σκέλος

σκέπτεσθαι

σκεπτῐκός

σκηνή

σκίουρος

σκληρός

σκολίωσις

σκοποῦ

σοφός

σπᾶν

σπασμός

σπᾰστῐκός

σπεῖρα

σπείρω

σπέρμα

σπήλαιον

σπῆλυγξ

σπλήν

σπορά̄

σπόρος

στάσις

στᾰτῐκός

στᾰτός

στέλλω

Στέντωρ

στερεός

στήλη

στίγμα

στίζειν

στίχος

στοά̄

στόμα

στρατηγία

στρᾰτηγός

στρατός

στρεπτός

στρέφειν

στροφή

στρῶμα

στῦλος

συμβάλλειν

σῠμπόσῐον

σύμπτωσις

σύν

συνάγειν

σῠνᾰγωγή

σῠνθεσῐς

σῠνοψῐς

σῠνώνῠμος

σύριγξ

συστέλλειν

σφαῖρα

σφυγμός

σφύζειν

σφῠξῐς

σχῆμα

σχίζω

σχίσις

σχιστός

σῶμα

σώφρων

τάγμᾰ

τάξις

τᾰσῖς

τάσσειν

ταῦρος

ταὐτο

τᾰφος

ταχύς

τείνειν

τέκτων

τελέω

τέλος

τέμνειν

τετανός

τέτταρες

τέφρα

τέχνη

τῆλε

τί

τιθέναι

το

το αἷμα

τόμος

τόνος

τόξον

τόπος

τρᾰπεζα

τραῦμα

τραχύς

τρέπειν

τρέφειν

τρέχειν

τρῆμα

τρηματώδης

τρι-

τρόπου

τροφή

τροχός

τύμπᾰνον

τυπικός

τύπος

τύπτειν

τύραννος

ὕαινα

ὑγιής

ὑγρός

ὕδρα

ὕδωρ

ὕλη

ὑπέρ

ὕπνος

ὑπό

ὑπόθεσις

ὑπόκρῐσῖς

ὕστέρᾱ

φαγεῖν

φαινόμενον

φάναι

φᾰντᾱσῐ́ᾱ

φᾰ́ντᾱσμᾰ

φάρμακον

φᾰ́σῐς

φέρειν

φήμη

φημί

φήρ

φθέγγεσθαι

φθόγγος

φιλία

Φῐ́λῐππος

φίλος

φλέγειν

φλέγμᾰ

φλέψ

φλόξ

φόβος

φορά

φόρησις

φράτηρ

φρήν

φυή

φῡλή

φύλλον

φῦλον

φυσικός

φύσις

φυτόν

φῠ́ω

φωνή

φῶς, φωτός

φωσφόρος

χαίρω

χᾰλκός

χαρά

χᾰρᾰκτήρ

χάρις

χᾰ́ρῐσμᾰ

χάρμα

χείρ

χήρ

χίλιοι

χλωρός

χολή

χόνδρος

χορδή

χορεία

χορός

χρόνος

χρῡσαλλίς

χρῡσός

χρῶμα

ψάλλειν

ψευδής

ψύχειν

ψυχή

ᾠόν

ὦτα

ωχρός

ὤψ

Printed in Great Britain
by Amazon

35948930R00094